# MACMILLAN/McGRAW-HILL

# Language Arts

6-Trait Writing

## Study Guide and Practice

Pages T2-T16

# 6-Trait Writing

## Study Guide and Practice

**Here are six key tools that help make your writing clearer.**

- **Ideas and Content**
- **Organization**
- **Sentence Fluency**
- **Voice**
- **Word Choice**
- **Conventions**

## Ideas and Content

### Is your writing clear and detailed?

Your **ideas** are the heart of your writing. **Details** help explain your ideas. Details show the reader what you think, feel, see, imagine, or know about your topic.

## TIPS FOR BETTER WRITING

- Be sure to gather enough information.

- Use interesting details that will make your piece fun to read.

- Be sure to *show* what is happening ("The sky got dark, and rain hit my face.") rather than *telling* what happened ("The storm began.").

Read Casey's **explanatory letter** to his pen-pal. Are his ideas clear?

Dear Lisa,

I started school yesterday, and now I have to go to bed early.

School starts at 7 A.M., so I get up early. That means my bedtime is early, too. I have a new bed.

Still, I like school, even if I cannot stay up late.

Your friend,

Casey

*The writer is writing about something he knows well.*

*This detail has nothing to do with the main idea.*

*The ending should add more information to the piece.*

**THINK AND WRITE**

- How can you make sure you keep your readers interested?
- Casey *tells* his pen-pal he is happy at his school. How can he *show* he is happy?

T3

# Writing

## Organization

**Is your writing well planned and easy to follow?**

**Organization** is the **plan** or **pattern** you choose to put your ideas and details in order.

### TIPS FOR BETTER WRITING

- Your beginning should grab the reader's attention and hint at what's coming.

- All your details should add a little more information to your main idea.

- Make sure to give the reader enough information, but not too much. If you give too little, the reader will get bored. If you give too much, the reader might get confused and miss the point.

- Your ending should give the reader something to think about.

This is Maria's **personal narrative**. Do you think it is well-organized?

My family went to the beach.
It was a fun day.
First, we made a sand castle.
Then, we swam. ~~My brother is on the swim team in his high school.~~
After that, we had fish for dinner.
I liked the beach so much that I want to go back.

*The first sentence tells what the story is about.*

*This sentence is not part of the main idea.*

*Maria put ideas in time order.*

**THINK AND WRITE**

- Why is it important to organize your ideas before you write?
- What words does Maria use to tell us the order of what happened?

# Writing

## Sentence Fluency

Do you like the way
your writing sounds when
it is read aloud?

When you write, your sentences need to make sense, and they should fit together easily.

### TIPS FOR BETTER WRITING

- Check that your writing is easy to read aloud. It should sound natural.

- Rewrite sentences that are hard to read aloud. Cut any extra words.

- Try using both long and short sentences.

- Find different words to begin each sentence.

Here is Timmy's **description**. Is it easy to read aloud?

**Writing**

The Grand Canyon is an interesting place. ~~To visit.~~

The canyon looks very big.

~~The canyon~~ It is many miles long.

There are ~~The canyon has~~ colored rocks.

At the bottom, there is a very big river ~~the river that~~ looks very small from the top of the canyon, but it is over 1,450 miles long.

> Combine these sentences.

> Try not to begin every sentence the same way.

> Run-on sentences make a paper hard to follow.

**THINK AND WRITE**

- Read Timmy's paper out loud. Write down the sentences that are hard to read out loud.

- How can you rewrite the sentences to make them sound better?

# Voice

## Do you shine through in your writing?

Your paper should sound different from the way anyone else writes. When people read your paper, they should feel that you are talking right to them.

## TIPS FOR BETTER WRITING

- Write about what you know and what you really care about.
- Be sure to write as if you are talking to another person.
- Don't be afraid to say what you really think.
- Write so the reader will feel just what you feel.

Look at Selma's **story**. Do you think she had fun writing it?

Some people were making a tired old cow pull heavy things.

> The writer has a clear picture in her head.

These people were only thinking of themselves.

> It is all right to say what you feel.

A little girl told them that they were being mean. So they gave her the cow. When she looked at the cow, the cow was smiling.

> The reader can tell how the writer feels about her story.

**THiNK AND WRITE**

- When a writer enjoys telling a story, does that change the story? How?

- What can you tell from her story about how Selma feels about animals?

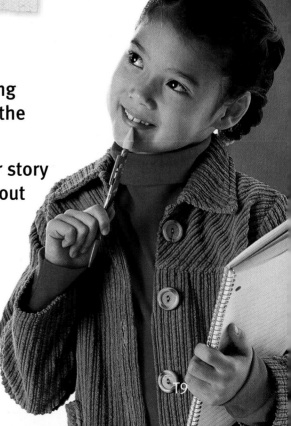

T9

# Writing

## Word Choice

**Do you choose words that create a picture in the reader's mind?**

Good **word choices** paint clear pictures in the reader's mind. They also help move the reader to feel and think the way you do.

### TIPS FOR BETTER WRITING

- Use nouns that clearly name a person, place, or thing. (A word like *nap* or *rest* is better than *sleep*.)

- Choose verbs that show the reader exactly what the action is. (The words *shouted*, *screamed*, or *roared* are better than *yelled*.)

- Choose describing words that tell the reader exactly how something looks, sounds, feels, tastes, or smells.

- Try to paint pictures so clearly that they stick in the reader's mind.

- Try not to use the same words over and over again.

This is a draft of Eddie's **expository paper**. Where can he improve his word choice?

loved

John Muir cared a lot about

plants, trees, and animals. He was
nature

upset that people hurt pretty

parts of the country.

John Muir told President
beautiful

Roosevelt that pretty places

should not be hurt by people.

Roosevelt agreed and made a law

to protect some pretty parks.

> Use interesting verbs.

> One word can replace many.

> Try not to use the same word many times.

 **THINK AND WRITE**

• How does a writer's word choice make her or his ideas clearer?

• What tools could Eddie use to help him find more interesting words?

## Conventions

**Did you revise and proofread your writing carefully?**

Here's an easy way for you to remember what to look for when you are proofreading your work: **CUPPS**. That stands for **C**apitalization, **U**sage, **P**unctuation, **P**aragraphs, and **S**pelling. These are the five **conventions** that need to be correct for your writing to be clear.

### TIPS FOR BETTER WRITING

- For help with rules for capitalization, see Handbook pages 448–450.

- Usage means the rules of English language. For help with rules for usage, see Troubleshooter pages 424–430 and Handbook pages 432–445.

- The rules for punctuation can be found in the Handbook pages 451–453.

- Check that your paragraphs develop only one main idea.

- For help with spelling rules and strategies, see Handbook pages 472–475.

Read Donna's paper that **compares** two sports. Do you see any errors?

Basketball and football are
both spots. Both are played
with a ball?

The games are very
different. Basketball is played
on a court. Football is played
on a field. A basketball is
round, and a Football Isn't.

*Check the spelling.*

*This sentence should end with a period.*

*These words should not be capitalized.*

**THINK AND WRITE**

- How does correct spelling help the reader?
- How could Donna proofread more carefully?

 # Writing

 # ✓Checklist

Use the checklist to help you
with your writing.

## PREWRITE

 **Ideas and Content**

❑ Do I know what I want to say?

❑ Do I need to research this topic?

 **Organization**

❑ Do I have a clear plan or pattern for my writing?

 **Voice**

❑ Am I really interested in the topic?

## DRAFT

 **Ideas and Content**

❑ Do I know the main idea or theme of my paper?

❑ Can I picture events or objects in my head?

 **Organization**

❑ Will the beginning grab the reader?

❑ Do I have an idea for the ending?

 **Voice**

❑ Do I know who I am writing for?

 **Word Choice**

❑ Do I know the meanings of any special words I plan to use in my writing?

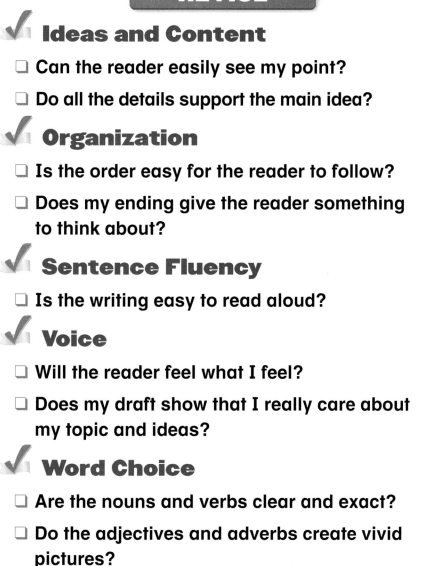

## REVISE

### ✓ Ideas and Content

- ❑ Can the reader easily see my point?
- ❑ Do all the details support the main idea?

### ✓ Organization

- ❑ Is the order easy for the reader to follow?
- ❑ Does my ending give the reader something to think about?

### ✓ Sentence Fluency

- ❑ Is the writing easy to read aloud?

### ✓ Voice

- ❑ Will the reader feel what I feel?
- ❑ Does my draft show that I really care about my topic and ideas?

### ✓ Word Choice

- ❑ Are the nouns and verbs clear and exact?
- ❑ Do the adjectives and adverbs create vivid pictures?

## PROOFREAD

### ✓ Conventions

- ❑ Have I checked my writing for correct **CUPPS**?

# Writing

**Presentation** is **how you share your writing**. It can be almost as important as what you have written. If your presentation is clear, your audience will want to pay attention. If it is not, your audience may be distracted from your message.

## TIPS FOR BETTER WRITING

- If you write by hand, make sure your lettering is easy to read.

- If you use a computer, choose a font that is easy to read. Be sure the margins and spacing are correct.

- Practice your presentation several times before you read it aloud.

- Consider using charts, graphs, pictures, headings, or photos to help make your meaning clear.

- Could you also present your information in the form of a photo essay, a play, a postcard, or something else?

**THINK AND WRITE**

- How might drawings make your ideas clearer?

- Why is good handwriting important?

# MACMILLAN/McGRAW-HILL
# Language Arts

The 6 Trait Writing rubric materials in this work use the Six Trait Writing criteria, as defined by the Northwest Regional Educational Laboratory. For more information, visit its website at www.nwrel.org.

**Contributor**

Time Magazine

Published by Macmillan/McGraw-Hill, of McGraw-Hill Education, a division of The McGraw-Hill Companies, Inc., Two Penn Plaza, New York, New York 10121.

Printed in the United States of America

ISBN 0-02-245559-0/2

2 3 4 5 6 7 8 9 (042/043) 08 07 06 05 04

# MACMILLAN/McGRAW-HILL
# Language Arts

**AUTHORS**

Jan E. Hasbrouck

Donna Lubcker

Sharon O'Neal

William H. Teale

Josefina V. Tinajero

Karen D. Wood

 Macmillan
McGraw-Hill

# UNIT 1

# Sentences and Personal Narrative

**Theme:** A New Day

**Grammar**  Spiral Review Every Day

## Sentences

### Build Skills

## Writing

### Personal Narrative

## Review and Assess

# UNIT 2

# Nouns and Descriptive Writing

**Theme:** *Person to Person*

## Grammar  *Spiral Review Every Day*

### Nouns

### Build Skills

## Writing

### Descriptive Writing

### Writing Process

### Present Your Descriptive Writing

## Review and Assess

# UNIT 3

# Verbs and Explanatory Writing

**Theme:** *Share with Us*

**Grammar**  *Spiral Review Every Day*

## Verbs

### Build Skills

## Writing

### Explanatory Writing

### Review and Assess

# Verbs and Writing That Compares

**Theme:** *What Do You Know?*

**Grammar**  *Spiral Review Every Day*

## Verbs

### Build Skills

x

## Writing

### Writing That Compares

### Review and Assess

# UNIT 5

# Pronouns and Expository Writing

**Theme:** *Ready...Plan...Go!*

## Grammar

 *Spiral Review Every Day*

### Pronouns

### Build Skills

## Writing

### Expository Writing

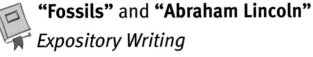
### Review and Assess

xii

# UNIT 6 Adjectives, Adverbs, and Writing a Story

**Theme:** New Directions

**Grammar**  Spiral Review Every Day

## Adjectives and Adverbs

## Writing

**A Story**

## Review and Assess

# Sentences and Personal Narrative

In this unit you will learn about sentences. You will also learn how to write a story about you.

**Social Studies Link** People enjoy telling stories about their lives. This writer is telling us about her childhood.

When I was young in the mountains, we pumped pails of water from the well at the bottom of the hill, and heated the water to fill round tin tubs for our baths.

from *When I Was Young in the Mountains* by Cynthia Rylant

## Thinking Like a Writer

**Personal Narrative**
A personal narrative tells a story about the writer's own life.

- How do you think Cynthia Rylant feels about her childhood?

**Sentences** Every sentence has a subject that tells who or what does something.

**QUICK WRITE** Write the words that tell who does something in each sentence.

# Sentences

**RULES**

A **sentence** tells a complete thought.

**My new puppy jumped out of the box.**

A group of words that does not tell a complete thought is not a sentence.

**My new puppy.**

A sentence names the person or thing you are talking about. It also tells what happened.

**My new puppy jumped out of the box.**

*what*      *what happened*

**THINK AND WRITE**

**Sentences**

What makes a group of words a sentence? Write the answer in your journal.

## Guided Practice

**Tell if each group of words is a sentence.**

**1.** We see four kittens.

**2.** Two little rabbits.

**3.** My sister wants a turtle.

**4.** Some goldfish.

**5.** The snake is sleeping.

## REVIEW THE RULES

- A sentence tells a complete thought.

- A group of words that does not tell a complete thought is not a sentence.

## More Practice

**A. Write only the complete sentences.**

6. The puppy licks my face.

7. Maria likes the kitten.

8. A loud squawk.

9. Inside the cage.

10. Alex names the bird Tweet.

**B.** Spiral Review **Add words to each group to make a complete sentence. Write the sentences.**

11. The white mice.

12. The tan puppy.

13. The hamster.

14. The little kittens.

15. The big dog.

**Handbook**
page 432

**Extra Practice**
page 58

**Writing Activity** Sentences

Write three sentences about a pet you would like.
**APPLY GRAMMAR:** Is each sentence complete?

Science Link

3

# Statements and Questions

## RULES

Every sentence begins with a capital letter. A **statement** is a sentence that tells something. It ends with a period.

**The girls are going to school.**

A **question** is a sentence that asks something. It ends with a question mark.

**Are the girls going to school?**

What kind of sentence is each?

**We live in the city.** $\longrightarrow$ statement
**Do you live in the city?** $\rightarrow$ question

**THINK AND WRITE**

**Sentences**
In your journal write how a statement and a question are different.

## Guided Practice

**Read each sentence. Tell if it is a statement or a question.**

**1.** Where is your new neighborhood?

**2.** We moved to the city.

**3.** Do you live in a house?

**4.** I live in an apartment.

**5.** I hope I meet new friends.

## REVIEW THE RULES

- A **statement** is a sentence that tells something. It ends with a period.

- A **question** is a sentence that asks something. It ends with a question mark.

## More Practice

**A.** **Write the sentences. Underline each statement. Circle each question.**

**6.** Why did your family move?

**7.** Mom got a new job.

**8.** Will you visit my new neighborhood?

**9.** A nice family lives next door.

**10.** I made two new friends.

**B.** **Spiral Review** **Write each complete sentence.**

**11.** Can we visit next week?

**12.** My dad will drive us.

**13.** Your new address.

**14.** We like the city.

**15.** Are the buildings tall?

**Handbook**
**page 432**

**Extra Practice**
**page 59**

### Writing Activity  Note

Write a friend a note about a building you saw.
**APPLY GRAMMAR:** Circle each end mark.

# Commands and Exclamations

## RULES

A **command** is a sentence that tells someone to do something. A command ends with a period.

**Come to the zoo with us.**

An **exclamation** is a sentence that shows strong feeling. An exclamation ends with an exclamation mark.

**What a funny monkey I saw!**

What kind of sentence is each?

**Read the sign.** ⟶ command

**That is a huge sign!** ⟶ exclamation

**THINK AND WRITE**

**Sentences**

How is a command different from an exclamation? Write the answer in your journal.

## Guided Practice

**Write each sentence. Then tell if each sentence is a command or an exclamation.**

**1.** Bring your camera along.

**2.** I am so excited!

**3.** Let me take your picture.

**4.** How big that elephant is!

**5.** Look for the baby gorilla.

---

**REVIEW THE RULES**

- A **command** tells someone to do something.

- An **exclamation** shows strong feeling.

---

## Practice

**A.** Write each sentence. Then write the letter C after each command.

**6.** Look at my map.

**7.** Help me find the lions.

**8.** What a long snake!

**9.** Take a picture of the tiger.

**10.** This zoo is great!

**B.** **Spiral Review** Write each sentence correctly. Then write *statement, question, command,* or *exclamation.*

**11.** The seals like to swim

**12.** Is the giraffe tall

**13.** Come see the brown bear

**14.** Where is the kangaroo

**15.** How big the zoo is

**Handbook**
page 432

**Extra Practice**
page 60

**Writing Activity** **Message**

Write a message to a zoo worker.
**APPLY GRAMMAR:** Use an exclamation mark.

7

# Sentence Punctuation

> ## RULES
>
> Begin every sentence with a capital letter.
>
> A **statement** ends with a period.
>
> A **question** ends with a question mark.
>
> A **command** ends with a period.
>
> An **exclamation** ends with an exclamation mark.

**Handbook**
pages 432, 451

**Extra Practice**
page 61

## Practice

**A. Begin and end each sentence correctly.**

**1.** tell me about the party

**2.** what a great party it was

**3.** we had so much fun

**4.** did you see the gifts

**5.** tara gave Steve a book

**B.** **Spiral Review** **Write each sentence correctly. Then write *statement*, *question*, *command*, or *exclamation*.**

**6.** we played some party games

**7.** how many games do you know

**8.** teach me a new game

**9.** there were so many balloons

**10.** did you get a balloon

**Sentences**
Does reading a sentence out loud help you choose the right end mark? How? Write your answer in your journal.

8

# Sentences

## REVIEW THE RULES

- A **sentence** tells a complete thought. A sentence always begins with a capital letter.

- A **statement** tells something.

- A **question** asks something.

- A **command** tells or asks someone to do something.

- An **exclamation** shows strong feeling.

## QUICK WRITE

**Sentences**
Does using different kinds of sentences help your writing? How? Write your ideas.

## Practice

**A.** Tell what kind of sentence each group of words is.

1. My family planted a garden.

2. What fun we all had!

3. How do you plant seeds?

4. Come and see our sunflowers.

5. Take a walk in our garden.

**B.** **Challenge** Rewrite the paragraph using the correct end marks.

**6.–10.** A garden needs care? There are seeds to plant. What seeds do you have! Help us pull out weeds. What a hard job.

# Subjects in Sentences

## RULES

The **subject** of a sentence tells who or what does something.

**The jet sits on the runway.**

Look at who this sentence is telling about.

**Gail goes to the airport.**

↑

subject

**THiNK AND WRITE**

**Sentences**

Why is the subject an important part of a sentence? Write the answer in your journal.

## Guided Practice

**Name the subject in each sentence.**

**1.** Many people fill the airport.

**2.** The airport is a busy place.

**3.** Airplanes are coming and going.

**4.** Gail sees a big jet.

**5.** A pilot walks to the plane.

10

## REVIEW THE RULES

- The **subject** of a sentence tells who or what does something.

## More Practice

**A. Write each sentence. Underline the subject.**

6. The airport is near the city.

7. Mom drives to the airport.

8. A man checks our tickets.

9. The plane will take off soon.

10. My whole family likes to fly.

**B.** [Spiral Review] **Write each complete sentence. Circle each subject.**

11. That airplane is huge!

12. Workers check the plane.

13. One worker looks at the wings.

14. The big suitcases.

15. Many people fly on the jet.

**Handbook**
page 433

**Extra Practice**
page 62

## Writing Activity  A Journal Entry

Write a journal entry about a place you would like to visit. Remember to begin each sentence in a different way.
**APPLY GRAMMAR:** Underline each subject.

# Predicates in Sentences

**RULES**

The **predicate** in a sentence tells what the subject does or what it is.

**The park** is large.

What do the people do in this sentence?

**People jog in the park.**

↑
predicate

**THINK AND WRITE**

**Sentences**

Why do sentences need subjects and predicates? Write the answer in your journal.

## Guided Practice

**Name the predicate in each sentence.**

**1.** The park is nice and clean.

**2.** People use the park each day.

**3.** Emma walks her dog.

**4.** Two children play ball.

**5.** The park closes at night.

- The **predicate** tells what the subject does or is.

## More Practice

**A. Write each sentence. Underline the predicate.**

**6.** A child sits on the grass.

**7.** The park bench is full .

**8.** We run to the duck pond .

**9.** Ben feeds some birds.

**10.** Two squirrels run up a tree .

**B.** **Spiral Review** **Write each sentence. Circle the subject. Underline the predicate.**

**11.** Everyone likes the park .

**12.** Some children play tag .

**13.** Two boys fly kites .

**14.** A woman sells peanuts.

**15.** Many people ride their bikes .

**Handbook**
page 433

**Extra Practice**
page 63

### Writing Activity   A Poem

Write a poem about a park or the outdoors.
**APPLY GRAMMAR:** Underline each predicate.

# Combining Sentences

## RULES

You can put two sentences together if they have the same predicate.

Use the word **and** to join the sentences.

**Rosa ran fast.    Mike ran fast.**
**Rosa** and **Mike ran fast**

See which words in the two sentences are the same. See which words can be put together with *and*.

**Rosa** saw a parade. **Mike** saw a parade.

**Rosa** and **Mike** saw a parade.

**THINK**
**AND WRITE**

**Sentences**

Why do writers combine sentences? Write the answer in your journal.

## Guided Practice

**Use *and* to join each pair of sentences.**

**1.** Boys marched. Girls marched.

**2.** Horns blew. Whistles blew.

**3.** Dave clapped. Lisa clapped.

**4.** Flags flew. Banners flew.

**5.** Drums played. Flutes played.

---

**REVIEW THE RULES**

- You can join two sentences if they have the same predicate.

- Use the word *and* to join the sentences.

---

## Practice

**A.** **Use the word *and* to join each pair of sentences. Write the new sentences.**

**6.** Elephants marched. Horses marched.

**7.** Men sang. Women sang.

**8.** Clowns passed by. Floats passed by.

**9.** Fran laughed. Jake laughed.

**10.** Sally cheered. Roger cheered.

**B.** Spiral Review **Write each sentence. Add the correct end mark. Circle the subject.**

**11.** A clown sang and danced

**12.** Dad and I took pictures

**13.** I never laughed so hard before

**14.** We clapped and shouted

**15.** That clown was so funny

**Handbook**
page 433

**Extra Practice**
page 64

### Writing Activity   A Paragraph

Write a paragraph about a class event.
**APPLY GRAMMAR:** Use *and* to join sentences.

15

# Commas in a Series

**Grammar**

> **RULES**
>
> Use **commas** to separate three or more words in a series or group.
>
> **Billy, Lee, and I visited the farm.**

## Practice

**A.** Tell where the commas go in each group of words.

**1.** cat dog and pony

**2.** Lucy Sam and Roy

**3.** horses cows and goats

**4.** hens chicks and roosters

**5.** house barn and shed

**B.** Spiral Review Write each sentence. Circle the subject. Underline the predicate.

**6.** The cows and sheep eat grass.

**7.** The farmer picks lots of corn.

**8.** The baskets are really full!

**9.** Tom, Len, and I rake the hay.

**10.** The farm is a great place!

**Handbook**
**page 452**

**Extra Practice**
**page 65**

**THiNK AND WRITE**

**Sentences**

How do commas in a series help make the sentence clear? Write your answer.

# Sentences

> **REVIEW THE RULES**
>
> - The **subject** of a sentence tells who or what does something.
>
> - The **predicate** tells what a subject does or is.
>
> - Use *and* to join two sentences that have the same predicate.
>
> - Use **commas** to separate words in a series.

## Practice

**A.** **Write each sentence. Circle each subject. Underline each predicate. Add commas to separate words in a series.**

**Handbook**
**page 433**

1. Uncle Ty made sandwiches.

2. Aunt Lu cut up a watermelon.

3. Ashley mixed the lemonade.

4. Bees ants and flies may come, too!

5. Sam Al and Jo got a basket.

**B.** **Challenge** **Write each pair of sentences as one sentence. Use *and.***

**Sentences**
**What do you know about sentences? Write your ideas in your journal.**

6. Todd brought fruit. Lee brought fruit.

7. Adam ate salad. Mia ate salad.

8. Mom cooked outside. Dad cooked outside.

9. Grandma had fun. Grandpa had fun.

10. Sam carried the bag. Al carried the bag.

# Common Errors with Incomplete Sentences

A sentence must tell a complete thought. Sometimes writers make a mistake.

| Common Errors | Examples | Corrected Sentences |
|---|---|---|
| The sentence has no predicate. | My turtle. | My turtle lives in a pond. |
| The sentence has no subject. | Swam away. | The ducks swam away. |

## THINK AND WRITE

**Sentences**

How do you know if a sentence is not complete? Write the answer in your journal.

**Troubleshooter**
**pages 420–421**

— REVIEW THE RULES —

**SENTENCES**

- Every complete sentence has a **subject** and a **predicate**.

- Every sentence begins with a capital letter and ends with a punctuation mark.

## Practice

**Write each complete sentence.**

**1.** The children.

**2.** We saw two goats.

**3.** Ran quickly.

**4.** The goats ate grass.

**5.** My dog barked at them .

# Mechanics and Spelling

## Directions

Read the paragraph and decide which type of mistake appears in each underlined part. Choose the correct answer.

---

**Sample**

Mama bird sat on the eggs in the nest. <u>she</u> **(1)**
<u>kept them very warm</u>. Soon the eggs began to
crack. <u>Out popped baby birds</u>? They opened **(2)**
their mouths wide. <u>Mama bird heard their crys</u>. **(3)**
Baby birds are very hungry!

> *See if every sentence begins with a capital letter.*

> *Is this a statement or a question? Make sure the end mark is correct.*

> *Check all the underlined words for mistakes in spelling.*

---

**1** ○ Spelling
  ○ Capitalization
  ○ Punctuation

**3** ○ Spelling
  ○ Capitalization
  ○ Punctuation

**2** ○ Spelling
  ○ Capitalization
  ○ Punctuation

> **Test Tip**
> Read the underlined parts slowly and carefully.

19

**RESEARCH**

## RESEARCH When I do research and read a word I don't know, I look it up in the **dictionary**. The dictionary helps me explain new words to my readers. The more research I do, the more words I learn. In this photo essay, I wrote about Michael Jordan's decision to retire. Do you know what <u>retire</u> means?

**COMPOSITION SKILLS**

## WRITING WELL When I write, I use **paragraphs** to help put together my thoughts. In this photo essay, each paragraph tells something different about Michael Jordan.

**VOCABULARY SKILLS**

## USING WORDS Words like <u>first</u>, <u>middle</u>, and <u>last</u> are **time-order words**. They tell about the order in which things happen. Time-order words help my readers keep track of the events I'm writing about.

# Read Now!

Find out more about Michael Jordan. As you read, write down the important information in each paragraph.

# TIME FOR KIDS

## PHOTO ESSAY

# Michael Jordan

**A great athlete says good-bye to basketball.**

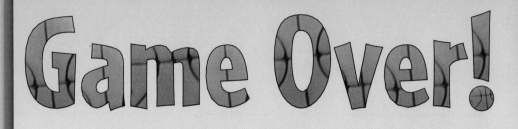

# Game Over!

Mike Powell/Allsport; inset photo: John W. McDonough

**M**ichael Jordan is one of the greatest basketball players of all time. Jordan led his team, the Chicago Bulls, to six world championships. He was one of the highest scorers in basketball history.

In 1993, Jordan first decided to retire. But he changed his mind and returned to the Bulls. Then in 1999, Jordan quit a second time. He said, "I'm just going to enjoy life. I'm going to do some of the things I've never done before."

What's next for Jordan? He wants to spend time with his family. He wants to watch his kids play one-on-one basketball.

Everyone knows Michael Jordan's big smile.

Cover: John Biever/Sports Illustrated
Michael S. Green/AP

**inter NET CONNECTION** Go to www.mhschool.com/language-arts for more information on the topic.

John Biever/Sports Illustrated

Jordan won two gold medals at the Olympic Games. He won the first in 1984. He won the second in 1992.

Jordan's basketball number was 23. It may be the best known basketball number in the world.

# Write Now!

Everyone is good at something. Michael Jordan was very good at playing basketball. Think about something that you are good at. Write to tell about it.

23

# The Dictionary

A **dictionary** is a book that tells what words mean. The words the dictionary tells about are called **entry words**. All the entry words are in ABC order.

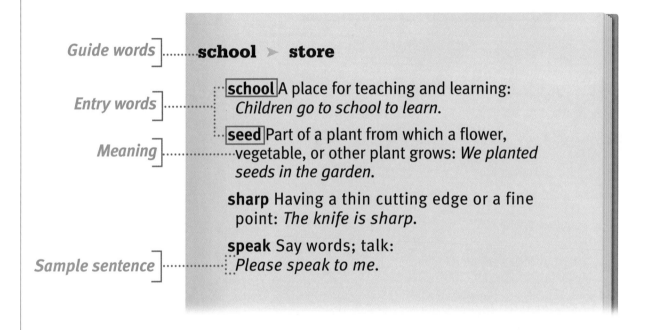

Guide words ........ **school** ➤ **store**

Entry words ..........

Meaning ..............

school  A place for teaching and learning: *Children go to school to learn.*

seed  Part of a plant from which a flower, vegetable, or other plant grows: *We planted seeds in the garden.*

sharp  Having a thin cutting edge or a fine point: *The knife is sharp.*

speak  Say words; talk: *Please speak to me.*

Sample sentence ..........

Each dictionary page has two **guide words** at the top. The guide word on the left tells what the first word on the page is. The guide word on the right tells the last word on the page.

Some words have a **sample sentence**. It shows how the word is used.

## Practice

**A. Use the dictionary page on page 24 to answer.**

**1.** Name the two guide words on the page.

**2.** Which guide word shows the *first* word?

**3.** Which guide word shows the *last* word?

**4.** What does the word *school* mean?

**5.** Which word comes after the word *seed*?

**B. Complete each sentence with a word or words from the box.**

**inter NET**
**CONNECTION**

**Go to**
www.mhschool.
com/language-arts

**for more
information
on using the
dictionary.**

```
dictionary      guide word    sample sentence
entry words     ABC order
```

**6.** The _____ tells the meanings of many words.

**7.** The dictionary gives meanings for the_____.

**8.** The entry words are listed in _____ .

**9.** The first _____ tells the first entry word on the page.

**10.** The _____ shows how to use the entry word.

### Writing Activity  Use a Dictionary

Use the dictionary on pages 480–495 to write the guide words on the same page as *butterfly*. Write the meaning of *butterfly*.

# Vocabulary: Time-Order Words

**THiNK AND WRITE**

**Time-Order Words and Phrases**

How can time-order words make your writing clearer? Write your answer in your journal.

---

**DEFINITION**

Time-order words show the order in which things happen.

### Time-Order Words and Phrases

| | | |
|---|---|---|
| first | after | yesterday |
| next | before | today |
| then | now | tomorrow |
| finally | soon | long ago |

---

Look at the blue time-order words and phrases in this paragraph.

*Today* our class took a trip to the zoo. *First* we looked at animals in the reptile house. *Next* we went outside to see the bears and big cats. *Then* we stopped to eat lunch. *After* lunch, we went into the bird house. *Last of all*, we stopped at the gift shop.

## Practice

**A.** **Write each sentence. Circle time-order words.**

**1.** Yesterday we talked about the zoo.

**2.** Today we visited the zoo.

**3.** We had questions before our trip.

**4.** After our trip, we knew the answers.

**5.** We will write about the trip tomorrow.

**B.** **Copy these sentences in the right order.**

**6.** Finally we drove to the zoo.

**7.** Next we sat down in our seats.

**8.** Then the driver started the bus.

**9.** First we got on the bus.

**10.** Soon the driver climbed in.

**C.** **Grammar Link** **Complete each sentence with a word from the box. Use capital letters correctly.**

| long ago | then | now | soon | last month |
|---|---|---|---|---|

**11.** _____ zoo animals lived in cages.

**12.** _____ they live in open spaces.

**13.** _____ the zoo added more animals.

**14.** I want to go to the zoo _____ .

**15.** _____ I can see the new panda.

**Writing Activity** **Sentences**

Write about a school event. Use time-order words.
**APPLY GRAMMAR:** Be sure to use correct punctuation.

27

# Composition: Paragraphs

Good writers put their ideas in paragraphs to make their writing clearer.

---

**GUIDELINES**

- A **paragraph** is a group of sentences that all tell about **one idea**.

- The first sentence of a paragraph is indented or moved in.

---

**THINK AND WRITE**

**Paragraphs**

How does putting writing in paragraphs make it easier to understand?

Look at how the first sentence is indented in this paragraph. Notice that all the sentences tell about one idea.

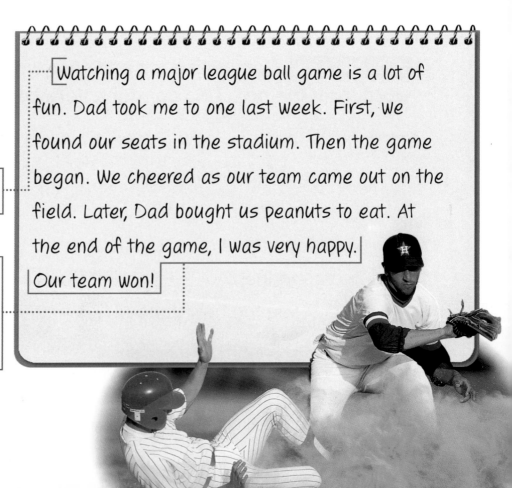

*The paragraph is indented.*

Watching a major league ball game is a lot of fun. Dad took me to one last week. First, we found our seats in the stadium. Then the game began. We cheered as our team came out on the field. Later, Dad bought us peanuts to eat. At the end of the game, I was very happy. Our team won!

*All the sentences tell about watching a major league ball game .*

## Practice

**A.** **Write each sentence. Write *yes* if it belongs in a paragraph about soccer.**

**1.** We played soccer last week.

**2.** I scored a goal in the game.

**3.** Baseball is a lot of fun.

**4.** My team won the soccer game.

**5.** I bought a new baseball.

**B.** **Write a beginning sentence for a paragraph about each topic.**

**6.** My Favorite Game

**7.** Fun on the Playground

**8.** Sports on Television

**9.** Famous Athletes

**10.** Exercise Is Good for You

**C.** **Grammar Link** **11.–15. Read each sentence you just wrote. Add another sentence that tells more about the topic.**

### Writing Activity   A Paragraph

Write a paragraph about a game you play with your friends. Indent the paragraph.
**APPLY GRAMMAR:** Make sure each sentence has a subject and predicate.

# Better Sentences

## Directions

Read the paragraph. Some parts are underlined. The underlined parts may be one of the following:

- Incomplete sentences
- Correctly written sentences that should be combined

Choose the best way to write each underlined part.

---

**Sample**

Dogs are not just pets. <u>Many dogs work</u>.
(1)
<u>Many dogs help people</u>. There are seeing-eye dogs who help people who are blind. There are dogs who pull sleds over ice and snow. Some dogs work on farms and help round up sheep. <u>Help catch criminals</u>. Dogs can be good workers
(2)
as well as special friends.

*Check to see if two short sentences can be combined to make one sentence.*

*Look out for a group of words that does not tell a complete thought.*

---

**1** ○ Many dogs work many help people.

○ Many dogs and many people help.

○ Many dogs work and help people.

**2** ○ Police dogs help catch criminals.

○ Help catch criminals for them.

○ Dogs to help catch criminals.

*Test Tip*
**Read the underlined words and phrases carefully.**

# Vocabulary and Comprehension

## Directions

Read the paragraph. Then read each question that follows the paragraph. Choose the best answer to each question.

**Sample**

I remember the day I learned to ride a bike. I was afraid of falling, but my big sister held onto me. She ran along beside me. I loved the wind against my face. I wanted to go faster. So I pushed my legs harder and forgot about my sister. The next thing I knew, I was riding all by myself! I was very proud. The only problem was that I didn't know how to stop. <u>Finally</u>, I had to fall off the bike to make it stop. Ouch!

*Some words help you understand the order of when things happen.*

**1** How did the writer feel about learning to ride a bike?

○ sad

○ bored

○ proud

**2** The word <u>finally</u> in the story means—

○ in the end

○ at the start

○ before long

# Seeing Like a Writer

Pictures can give you ideas for your writing. Pretend you are in one of these pictures. Look at the details. How would you feel? What would you say about your experience?

*Carnival Time in Willow Bend* by Jane Wooster Scott.

## Writing from Pictures

1. What would you like to know about the pictures? Write a question for each picture.

2. Write what is happening in one of the pictures. Use time-order words.

3. Choose two pictures. How are they alike? Write a paragraph about those pictures.

**Apply Grammar:** Begin and end your sentences correctly. Circle each capital letter and end mark.

33

# Personal Narrative

A personal narrative can be a story about you. When you write a personal narrative, you tell what you did and how you felt.

### Learning from Writers

Read these personal narratives. Notice how the authors begin and end their stories.

**THiNK AND WRITE**

**Purpose**

Why do you think these authors wrote these stories?

## The Relatives Came

It was in the summer of the year when the relatives came. They came up from Virginia. They left when their grapes were nearly purple enough to pick, but not quite. The relatives stayed for weeks and weeks. They helped us tend the garden and they fixed any broken things they could find. They ate up all our strawberries and melons, then promised we could eat up all their grapes and peaches when we came to Virginia. But none of us thought about Virginia much. We were so busy hugging and eating and breathing together.

— Cynthia Rylant from *The Relatives Came*

# The Skunk Family

Once there was a skunk family that lived near my house. At first, I thought they were cute. But one night as we were driving home, a skunk ran in front of our car.

A few nights later, my dad, my dog Jerome, and I were taking a walk. I saw a skunk. It sprayed Jerome. The smell was so bad that it made my eyes and nose burn. The next night the skunk sprayed Jerome again. Now I know the skunk family isn't cute at all.

— Chris Barnes

## PRACTICE and APPLY

### Thinking Like a Reader

**1.** How does the author of "The Relatives Came" feel about her relatives?

**2.** What events took place in "The Skunk Family"? When did they happen?

### Thinking Like a Writer

**3.** What happens at the end of the first story?

**4.** What time-order words did you find in the second story?

**5. Reading Across Texts** Both personal narratives are about families. How are the two stories different?

# Features of a Personal Narrative

## DEFINITIONS AND FEATURES

A **personal narrative** tells about something that happened to you. A good personal narrative does these things:

▶ It tells a story from **personal experience**.

▶ It has a good **beginning** and **ending**.

▶ It uses **time-order words** to show that things happened in a certain order.

### ▶ Personal Experience

Reread "The Relatives Came" on page 34. Notice the words *our* and *we* in this sentence from the story. They tell us that it is about the author's own life.

> They ate up all our strawberries and melons, then promised we could eat up all their grapes and peaches when we came to Virginia.

### ▶ Good Beginning

See how the beginning of "The Relatives Came" catches our attention.

> It was in the summer of the year when the relatives came.

# A Surprise Picnic

by Sarah Brown

It was a special day. First, Dad woke us early. Next, we drove to Falls Lake. Then we found a shady spot under a big tree. Dad unpacked a picnic lunch. We ate sandwiches and drank lemonade. After lunch, we played catch in a grassy field. I had fun. It was nice to be with my family.

## PRACTICE and APPLY

**Plan Your Own Personal Narrative**

1. Check your revised draft one last time.

2. Make a neat, final copy.

3. Place your writing in a scrapbook. Add photos or drawings.

## TIP!

### TECHNOLOGY

Try different kinds of fonts for your title. Use a font that is large enough to stand out.

49

# Present Your Personal Narrative

You need to plan before you present your personal narrative.

**STEP 1**

## How to Tell Your Story

**Strategies for Speaking** Your purpose is to share your experiences with others as clearly as possible.

- Write the main events on a note card to help you remember.
- Make important points stand out by using body movements.
- Look at your audience. Smile.
- Speak so that everyone can hear you.

### Listening Strategies

- Have a purpose in mind as you listen.

- Picture the story in your mind.

- Watch the speaker for clues about feelings.

- Ask questions only at the end.

## Multimedia Ideas

You might want to play music. Find music that goes with your topic. Play it softly.

# How to Show Your Story
## Suggestions for Illustration

You can make your personal narrative more interesting with pictures.

- Show a scrapbook or a poster.
- Use souvenirs and drawings.
- Show a map of where things happened. Remember to label it.

# How to Share Your Story
## Strategies for Rehearsing

Practice your presentation before you give it.

- Watch yourself practice in a mirror.
- Have a partner listen and give ideas.
- Rehearse in front of a small group.

## Viewing Strategies

- Look carefully at each of the pictures and objects the speaker shows you.
- Read all the labels on the pictures.
- Look for details in the pictures.

## PRACTICE and APPLY
### Plan Your Own Personal Narrative

1. Make notes to help you remember.
2. Speak clearly and with feeling.
3. Show interesting pictures or objects.
4. Practice your personal narrative.

# Writing Tests

A writing test shows you a prompt to read and asks you to write something. A prompt gives you an idea and tells you what kind of writing to do. Look for key words and phrases that help you know what to write about and how to do your writing.

*Look for words that tell if the purpose is to entertain or inform.*

*Check to see if the prompt tells who the audience is.*

*Look for words that tell what kind of writing this is.*

> **Prompt**
>
> The first day of school can be a fun time.
> <u>Write a story</u> telling about <u>how you felt or what you did</u> on your first day at school.

## How to Read a Prompt

**Purpose**   Look back at the prompt. Find the words that tell you the purpose of the writing. The words "a fun time" and "write a story" tell you that your purpose will be to entertain.

**Audience**   Sometimes a prompt will tell you who the audience is. If it does not, think of your teacher as your audience.

**Personal Narrative**   When you are asked to write about something that happened to you, you are writing a personal narrative. The words "how you felt and what you did" tell you that you should write about your own experiences and feelings.

**Test Tip**
Read all the parts of a writing test slowly and carefully.

52

# Commas in a Series

**A. Write each group of words. Add commas where they belong.**

1. Mom Dad and I

2. clothes shoes and books

3. cars trucks and buses

4. bags suitcases and gifts

5. washer dryer and TV

6. windows doors and garage

7. dog cat and bird

8. Thursday Friday and Saturday

9. apples oranges and pears

10. pencils pens and crayons

**B. Write each sentence. Add commas where they belong.**

11. We drove past cities towns and farms.

12. We crossed plains hills and deserts.

13. The minutes hours and days flew by.

14. I bought gifts postcards and stamps.

15. I took pictures of Grandma Mom and Dad.

# Nouns and Descriptive Writing

In this unit you will learn about nouns. You will also learn how to describe things in your writing.

🔍 **Science Link**  Jamaica and Berto are building a sand castle. Can you picture it?

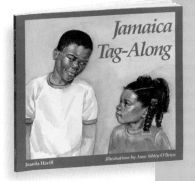

Jamaica sat down in the sand and began to dig. She made a big pile with the wet sand from underneath. She scooped sand from the mound to form a wall.

"Berto help," said the little boy. He sprinkled dry sand on the walls.

"Don't," said Jamaica. "You'll just mess it up."

〜 from ***Jamaica Tag-Along*** by Juanita Havill

## Thinking Like a Writer

**Descriptive Writing**
Descriptive writing tells what a person, place, or thing is like.

• What details help you picture the sand castle?

**Nouns** The author used nouns that name people, places, and things.

⏰ **QUICK WRITE** Write the nouns you find in the passage.

# Nouns

---

**RULES**

A **noun** is a word that names a person, place, or thing.

**My dog brings a bone into the house.**

Look at the nouns in the sentence below.

**My dad makes soup in the kitchen.**

↑      ↑      ↑

*person*     *thing*     *place*

---

**THINK AND WRITE**

**Nouns**

Look around the room. Write the names of five nouns you see.

## Guided Practice

**Name the noun in each sentence.**

**1.** The soup is warm.

**2.** The pot looks big.

**3.** My brother stirs.

**4.** My sister is hungry.

**5.** Our dog sits up and begs.

---

**REVIEW THE RULES**

- A **noun** names a person, place, or thing.

---

## More Practice

**A. Write each sentence. Then circle the noun.**

6. The yard is sunny.

7. My dad loves to cook!

8. The food is ready.

9. The chicken smells good.

10. The corn looks fresh.

**B. Spiral Review Write each sentence with the correct end mark. Then write *statement*, *question*, or *exclamation*.**

11. This restaurant is fun

12. Is our table ready

13. My friends are so happy

14. The food comes at last

15. Does the lunch taste good

**Handbook**
**page 434**

**Extra Practice**
**page 128**

**Writing Activity   Paragraph**

Write a paragraph about what the people in your home like to eat. Include interesting details.
**APPLY GRAMMAR:** Circle each noun.

# More About Nouns

## RULES

A **noun** can name a person, a place, or a thing.

**The children ride the bus to the park.**

Look at what each noun in the sentence above names.

| Person | Place | Thing |
|---|---|---|
| children | park | bus |

## THINK AND WRITE

**Nouns**

How can you tell if a word is a noun? Write your answer.

## Guided Practice

**Write the nouns in each sentence. Tell if each noun names a person, a place, or a thing.**

**1.** Our teacher has a backpack.

**2.** The driver is ready.

**3.** The bus goes down the street.

**4.** The children are happy.

**5.** The city is so noisy!

70

## REVIEW THE RULES

- A **noun** can name a person, a place, or a thing.

## More Practice

**A.** **Write each sentence. Circle nouns that name a person. Underline nouns that name places.**

6. The park has many trees.

7. A woman eats lunch by the pond.

8. A man catches a fish.

9. The children play on the swings.

10. Birds fly in the sky.

**B.**  **Spiral Review** **Write each sentence. Underline the subject. Circle each noun.**

11. My family visits the park.

12. My sister goes down the slide.

13. The boys sit on the grass.

14. Some fish swim in the pond.

15. Mom feeds the ducks.

**Handbook**
**page 434**

**Extra Practice**
**page 129**

### Writing Activity  Description

Write about a favorite place. Use details.
**APPLY GRAMMAR:** Circle each noun.

# Proper Nouns

**RULES**

Proper nouns name special people, pets, and places.

Aunt Lil **and** Patches **live on** Bay Street.

A proper noun begins with a capital letter.

| Nouns | Special Nouns |
|---|---|
| boy | Miguel |
| dog | Pepper |
| street | Elm Street |
| school | Hillside Day School |
| city | Riverside |

**THINK AND WRITE**

**Nouns**

Write in your journal how you can tell if a noun is a special noun.

## Guided Practice

**Write the nouns that need capital letters.**

**1.** My friend nick has a fish.

**2.** The fish's name is pippy.

**3.** I named my cat snowy.

**4.** We live on spring street.

**5.** Flora lives in newtown.

**REVIEW THE RULES**

- Nouns that name special people, pets, and places are proper nouns.

- A proper noun begins with a capital letter.

## More Practice

**A.** **Write each sentence. Begin each proper noun with a capital letter.**

6. My brother bill has a pet club.

7. I hope paul brings his dog.

8. The name of the dog is frisky .

9. My friend lisa has a rabbit.

10. The vet is in middletown .

**Handbook**
page 434

**Extra Practice**
page 130

**B.** **Spiral Review** **Write the sentences. Add commas. Circle each noun. Write if it names a person, place, or thing.**

11.–20. A dog  a cat  and a bird live at our house near the lake. My mother and sister really love our pets!

**Writing Activity** **Silly Story**

Write a silly story about a pet.
**APPLY GRAMMAR:** Include proper nouns.

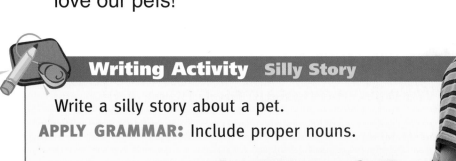

# Days, Months, and Holidays

## RULES

Some proper nouns name days of the week, months, and holidays.

The name of each day, month, and holiday begins with a capital letter.

**Is** Thanksgiving **on a** Thursday **in** November**?**

| Days | Months | | Holidays |
|---|---|---|---|
| Monday | January | July | Martin Luther |
| Tuesday | February | August | King Jr. Day |
| Wednesday | March | September | Memorial Day |
| Thursday | April | October | Thanksgiving |
| Friday | May | November | |
| Saturday | June | December | |
| Sunday | | | |

## THINK AND WRITE

**Nouns**

What kinds of words always begin with a capital letter? Write your answer.

## Guided Practice

**Write the nouns that need a capital letter.**

**1.** On tuesday everyone will get a part.

**2.** We will practice next friday.

**3.** We will make costumes in november.

**4.** Our play will be about thanksgiving.

**5.** Will we do a play in december?

74

---
**REVIEW** THE **RULES**
---

- Nouns that name days, months, and holidays begin with capital letters.

## More Practice

**A.** **Write each sentence. Begin each proper noun with a capital letter.**

**6.** We have a parade in january.

**7.** The parade is for new year's day.

**8.** We will practice on monday.

**9.** We will march on tuesday.

**10.** Is there a holiday in february?

**B.** **Spiral Review** **Write the sentences. Use capital letters and end marks correctly.**

**11.** My uncle lives in woodland

**12.** Is his farm on pine street

**13.** Uncle jim has a new pig

**14.** The pig's name is penny

**15.** Did they go to the woodland fair

**Handbook**
**page 435**

**Extra Practice**
**page 131**

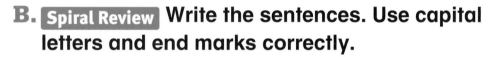

**Writing Activity** **A Poster**

Make a poster about a holiday or a special event.
**APPLY GRAMMAR:** Include three proper nouns.

**Social Studies Link**

# Using Capital Letters

Grammar

**Handbook**
pages 449-450

Extra
Practice
page 132

**Nouns**

What are some of your favorite special nouns? Write them correctly.

## RULES

Begin names of people, pets, and places with a capital letter.

**Jessica    Fluffy    Hilltop    Park**

The names of days, months, and holidays begin with capital letters.

**Monday    September    Labor Day**

### Practice

**A. Write each special noun that should have a capital letter.**

**1.** The next concert is on friday.

**2.** Uncle bob likes the music.

**3.** The band plays on main street.

**4.** Please come on july 4!

**5.** The band plays for independence day.

**B. Spiral Review Write each sentence. Add the end mark. Write *statement, question, command*, or *exclamation*.**

**6.** Max likes music

**7.** Max likes Monday, too

**8.** Does Max like the month of May

**9.** See Max on Memorial Day

**10.** Max loves the M Street Zoo

76

# Nouns

## REVIEW THE RULES

- A **noun** names a person, place, or thing.

- Nouns that name special people, pets, and places begin with capital letters.

- Nouns that name days, months, and holidays begin with capital letters.

## Practice

**Handbook**
pages 449–450

**A.** Write each sentence. Begin each proper noun with a capital letter.

**1.** What holidays are in february?

**2.** We celebrate presidents' day.

**3.** I wrote about abraham lincoln.

**4.** Does ann like valentine's day?

**5.** My sister likes groundhog day.

**B.** **Challenge** Write the paragraph. Fill in blanks with regular and proper nouns.

**6.–10.** My favorite holidays are _____ and my favorite place to celebrate is _____. I like to celebrate with _____ and _____.

**QUICK WRITE**

**Nouns**
How can you tell a regular noun from a special noun? Write your answer.

# Plural Nouns

## RULES

A **singular noun** names one person, place, or thing. A **plural noun** names more than one person, place, or thing.

**one singer    two singers**

Add **-s** to form the plural of most singular nouns.

**I know one song.**
**He knows two songs.**

Add **-es** to form the plural of nouns that end with *s, sh, ch,* or *x.*

**Put your box next to all the other boxes.**

**THINK AND WRITE**

**Nouns**

How can you tell if a noun is singular or plural? Write your answer.

## Guided Practice

**Make the noun in ( ) name more than one.**

**1.** Our (friend) have fun.

**2.** Two (boy) paint pictures.

**3.** Three (girl) play ball.

**4.** We find (bunch) of books.

**5.** One book is about (fox).

---

**REVIEW THE RULES**

- A **singular noun** names one person, place, or thing.

- A **plural noun** names more than one person, place, or thing.

---

## More Practice

**A.** **Make the noun in ( ) name more than one. Then write the new sentences.**

**6.** We need our (ruler) for math.

**7.** We measure in (inch).

**8.** Our class sings (song).

**9.** We write in our (journal).

**10.** We can tell about our (wish).

**Handbook**
page 436

**Extra Practice**
page 133

**B.** Spiral Review **Write each sentence. Underline the subject. Circle nouns for places.**

**11.** My mom and I visited the city.

**12.** We went to a museum.

**13.** The dinosaur room was crowded.

**14.** Mom saw a bookstore.

**15.** I chose a new book.

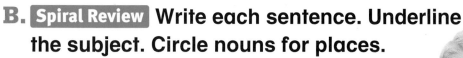

**Writing Activity** A Paragraph

Write a paragraph about something your class enjoys.
**APPLY GRAMMAR:** Include plural nouns and circle them.

# More Plural Nouns

**RULES**

To form the plural of nouns ending in a **consonant** and *y*, change *y* to *i* and add *-es*.

**bunny –y + i + es = bunnies**

Some nouns change their spelling to name more than one.

| Singular | Plural |
|----------|--------|
| man | men |
| woman | women |
| child | children |
| mouse | mice |
| foot | feet |

**THINK AND WRITE**

**Nouns**

Write how to change a noun ending in *-y* to show more than one.

## Guided Practice

**Change each noun in ( ) to make it name more than one person or thing.**

**1.** Three (woman) play music.

**2.** Some (man) sing songs.

**3.** Meg's two (foot) are flying!

**4.** Do the (pony) like the music?

**5.** All the (bunny) are asleep!

# Grammar and Usage

## Directions

**Read the paragraph and choose the word that belongs in each space.**

**Sample**

Frogs have long, strong back legs. In the water, the back __(1)__ kick and help the frog to swim quickly. On land a __(2)__ legs help it to jump and get away from danger. Some frogs can jump up high to catch __(3)__ flying by. Frogs have four legs, but the front legs are short. It's the back legs that do all the work.

*Look for nouns that are plural to match the verb <u>kick</u>.*

*Look for a noun that shows possession.*

*Check spelling. Add s to most nouns to show more than one.*

**1** ○ leg
   ○ legs
   ○ leg's

**2** ○ frog
   ○ frogs
   ○ frog's

**3** ○ insect's
   ○ insectss
   ○ insects

**Test Tip**
Always read the directions and the whole test carefully.

89

**RESEARCH**

**RESEARCH** When I do research or need to check information, the **library media center** is the first place I go. The books, magazines, newspapers, and computers there give lots of information. They help me write using correct information.

**COMPOSITION SKILLS**

**WRITING WELL** When I write, I make sure the **leads** that start my paragraphs will make readers want to read more. The **endings** that finish each paragraph tell my readers when I finish with an idea.

**VOCABULARY SKILLS**

**USING WORDS** Words like <u>grandmother</u> and <u>underground</u> are **compound words**. They are made from two separate words. When I write, I use them to explain a specific idea. What compound words do you know?

## Read Now!

As you read the photo essay about emeralds, jot down information that the writer could check in the library media center.

# EMERALDS

**They are green, beautiful, and very hard to find!**

# EMERALDS!

**J**ames Hill is very good at finding things hidden deep underground. It all started when he was a child. Back then, James visited his grandmother in Hiddenite, North Carolina. "First I crawled around her front yard," he says. Then he checked out the woods, creeks, and corn fields.

Wherever he went, he looked for buried treasure. One day, Hill discovered a real treasure in Hiddenite. It was a bed of emeralds. Emeralds are beautiful green gemstones.

Hill found the stones with his 8-year-old son. His son asked, "Daddy, did we find a treasure?" Hill told him, "Son, did we ever!"

When emeralds are polished, they become a beautiful shade of green. This necklace is made of emeralds and diamonds.

**inter NET CONNECTION** Go to www.mhschool.com/language-arts for more information on the topic.

This is how emeralds look when they are found.

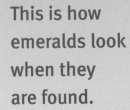

Necklace photo:Christies Images
All other photos:Warren F. Dobson/Full Moon Communications, N.C

Hill shows off his emerald. It will be cut and polished.

## Write Now!

James Hill and his son were surprised when they found emeralds in the ground. Describe a place where you once found a surprise.

93

# Note-taking and Summarizing

When you read a paragraph for information, you can take **notes**. The notes will help you remember what is most important about the paragraph. Read this paragraph about trees. Then read the notes that one student wrote.

**Trees**

There are many different kinds of trees. Each tree has its own kind of leaf. Sugar maple leaves have five large points. Elm leaves have zigzag edges. The leaves of the ginkgo tree are shaped like a fan.

**Notes**

Many kinds of trees

Different leaves

maple—5 points

elm—zigzag edges

ginkgo—like a fan

You can use your notes to write a **summary** that tells in a few sentences what the paragraph is about.

## Practice

**A. Use the notes on page 94 to answer these questions.**

1. What is the paragraph about?

2. What three different kinds of trees does the paragraph tell about?

3. What is a sugar maple leaf like?

4. What is an elm leaf like?

5. What is a ginkgo leaf like?

**B. Write the questions. Write the answer to each question.**

6. How does note-taking help you?

7. What should you look for when taking notes?

8. What can you use your notes to write?

9. Is a summary long or short?

10. Are the notes or the summary written in complete sentences?

**Writing Activity   A Summary**

Use the notes on page 94 to write a summary of the paragraph about trees.

# Vocabulary: Compound Words

## DEFINITION

A **compound word** is a word that is made from two smaller words. Knowing the meaning of the two smaller words can help you figure out the meaning of the compound word.

**birth + day = birthday**

**sea + shell = seashell**

**sun + light = sunlight**

**THINK AND WRITE**

**Compound Words**

How can compound words make your writing more interesting? Write your answer in your journal.

Look at the blue compound words below.

*Nature is all around me. Pretty bluebirds sing in my backyard. I see red ladybugs in Dad's vegetable garden. The air is filled with the sweet smell of wildflowers. The cool breeze fluffs up my dog's fur. Nature is everywhere.*

## ▶ Study Periodicals

Find magazine pictures of places that look like the one you are describing. The pictures can help you remember details. Read some of the articles. Look for describing words.

## Use Your Research

Add information from your research to your chart. This writer learned two new things.

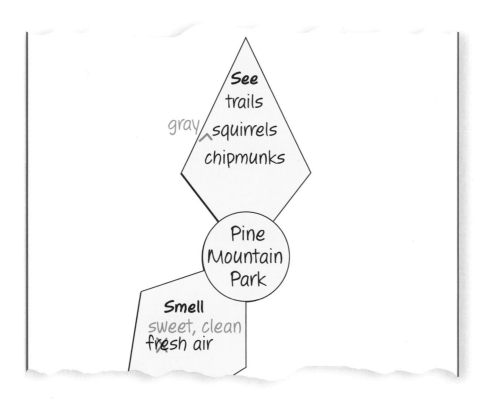

PREWRITE

DRAFT

REVISE

PROOFREAD

PUBLISH

**Handbook**
**pages 456–457**

## Checklist ✓

**Research and Inquiry**

■ Did you list your questions?

■ Did you find helpful resources?

■ Did you take notes or check out library materials?

## PRACTICE and APPLY

### Review Your Plan

**1.** Look at your prewriting chart.

**2.** List any questions you have.

**3.** Decide on resources that will help you.

**4.** Add new information to the chart.

# Draft

**Writing** PROCESS

You can write your description as a travel guide. Before you start, look at your star chart. Think about a main idea for the description. The details on your chart should tell about it.

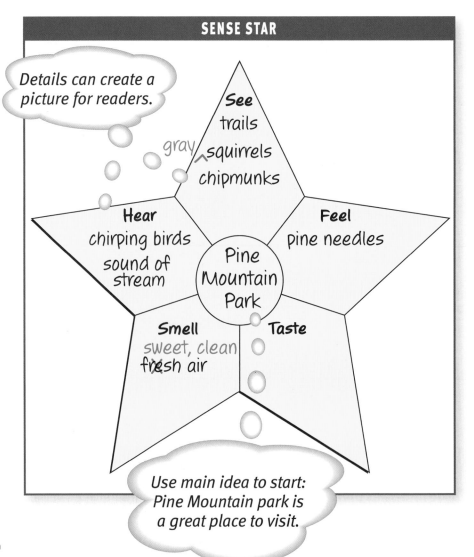

**SENSE STAR**

*Details can create a picture for readers.*

**See**
trails
gray squirrels
chipmunks

**Hear**
chirping birds
sound of stream

**Feel**
pine needles

Pine Mountain Park

**Smell**
sweet, clean fresh air

**Taste**

*Use main idea to start: Pine Mountain park is a great place to visit.*

✓ **Checklist**

**Drafting**

- Did you keep your purpose and your audience in mind?

- Did you use details to create pictures for the reader?

- Did you group the details in an order that makes sense?

- Did you include describing words?

# Come to Pine Mountain Park
## by Eric Parker

Pine Mountain Park is a great place to visit! There are miles of walking trails through green woods. You can see busy gray squirrels and chipmunks. You can hear birds chirping. A tiny stream makes bubbling noises. The air is sweet and clean. As you walk, you can feel pine needles crunch under your feet. Come visit soon!

PREWRITE

DRAFT

REVISE

PROOFREAD

PUBLISH

## PRACTICE and APPLY
### Publish Your Own Description

**1.** Check your revised draft once more.

**2.** Print or write a neat final copy.

**3.** Add drawings or photographs.

**4.** Make a cover for your travel guide.

**TIP!**

**Handwriting**
As you write, leave a lot of space around your words. This makes it easier to read.

119

# Present Your Descriptive Writing

**You need to plan before you present your description.**

## STEP 1

### How to Share Your Description

**Strategies for Speaking**

Your purpose is to make your audience want to visit the place you describe.

- Write your main idea and a few details on a note card to help you remember.
- Look at your audience. Smile.
- Make important points stand out by using body movements.
- Speak so that everyone can hear you.

**TiP!**

**Listening Strategies**

- Decide what you want to find out.
- Imagine what the speaker is describing.
- Keep your eyes on the speaker.
- Ask questions at the end of the talk.

## Multimedia Ideas

Do you have home videos of the place you are describing? If so, you might want to show them before or after you speak.

# How to Show Your Description

## Suggestions for Illustration

You can make what you have to say more interesting with pictures.

- Show photos or drawings of the place you describe.
- Point out the place on a map.
- If you have small pictures or souvenirs, pass them around.

# How to Share Your Travel Guide

## Strategies for Rehearsing Practice your presentation before you give it.

- Ask a partner to make suggestions.
- Watch yourself practice in a mirror.
- Tape-record your description. Listen to the tape. How can you make it better?

**Viewing Strategies**

- Study the pictures carefully.

- Look for details that the speaker does not tell you.

- Watch the speaker for clues about how he or she feels.

## PRACTICE and APPLY

### Present Your Own Descriptive Writing

1. Make notes to help you remember.

2. Look at your audience as you speak.

3. Use interesting pictures and objects.

4. Practice what you have to say.

# Writing Tests

On a writing test, you are given a prompt that asks you to write something. Remember to read the prompt carefully. Look for key words and phrases that tell you what to write about and how to do your writing.

> *Look for words that tell who the audience is.*

> *Look for words that tell if the purpose is to entertain or inform.*

> *Look for hints about what kind of writing this is.*

---

**Prompt**

   Think about what a room at home looks like.
   Write a paragraph <u>for your teacher</u> telling <u>what the room looks like</u> or <u>what you might see</u> in that room.

---

## How to Read a Prompt

**Purpose**   Read the prompt again. Look for the words that tell you the purpose of the writing. In this prompt, the words "what the room looks like" tell you that the purpose is to inform.

**Audience**   The prompt tells who the audience is. The words "for your teacher" let you know that your teacher is the audience.

**Descriptive Writing**   When you are asked to write about what a place looks like, you are writing a description. The words "looks like" and "what you might see" tell you that you should use describing words and details to show what the place is like.

**Test Tip**
If you do not understand a prompt, read it again carefully.

122

**Share your experiences with a pen pal** Wouldn't it be fun to have a pen pal from another country? Ask your teacher to help you join a pen-pal club, and choose someone to write a letter to.

Write your letter. Tell about your life at school and at home. Ask questions about your pen-pal's life.

## A Poster

If you were born in May, your birthstone is the emerald. Look in the encyclopedia for a list of the birthstones for each month.

**Birthstones** Create a poster about birthstones. Write a sentence or two about each stone. Use colorful words.

## Extra Practice

# Nouns

**A. Write the underlined words that are nouns.**

1. <u>Where</u> is the <u>birdhouse</u>?

2. <u>Look</u> in the <u>yard</u>.

3. The <u>grass</u> <u>is</u> dry.

4. <u>Find</u> the <u>hose</u>.

5. We <u>need</u> <u>seeds</u>.

6. Let's <u>go</u> to the <u>store</u>.

7. Where <u>are</u> the <u>keys</u>?

8. <u>Get</u> into the <u>truck</u>.

9. <u>Put</u> on your <u>seat belt</u>.

10. We <u>need</u> <u>birdseed</u>, too.

**B. Write each sentence. Then circle the noun.**

11. Do you see the nest?

12. Look up in the tree.

13. The birds are eating.

14. The branch sways.

15. Let's take a picture.

# More About Nouns

**A.** Write *person*, *place*, or *thing* to tell what each underlined noun names.

1. Where is my <u>flute</u>?

2. The <u>case</u> is empty!

3. Is it in the <u>kitchen</u>?

4. Did my <u>sister</u> take it?

5. My <u>teacher</u> just called.

6. I must learn a new <u>song</u>.

7. My <u>brother</u> helps me look.

8. We look all over the <u>house</u>.

9. We check my <u>bedroom</u> last.

10. I see it on my <u>desk</u>!

**B.** Write each sentence. Circle the noun that names a person or people. Underline nouns that name things.

11. My family likes music.

12. We go to concerts in the park.

13. My mom brings a blanket.

14. We watch the stars in the sky.

15. We listen to the music and crickets.

## Extra Practice

## Proper Nouns

**A.** **Write the proper nouns in the sentences.**
**Begin each proper noun with a capital letter.**

1. miss ames tells us about the new boy.

2. He will start school on tuesday.

3. His name is michael bono.

4. The bonos are from texas.

5. His family has just moved to seaside.

6. Our town is in florida.

7. The bonos live on shore drive.

8. Our house is on dune road.

9. I belong to a pet club called feathers.

10. michael has a pet parrot called henry.

**B.** **Write each sentence. Use capital letters correctly.**

11. Ask michael to join our pet club.

12. The club meets on friday.

13. My friend andy from bayside is coming.

14. The pet store is on main street.

15. The pet store owner is alan lee.

130

# Days, Months, and Holidays

**A.** Write the proper nouns that name days of the week, months, and holidays.

1. January is a busy month.

2. February is busy, too.

3. Groundhog Day comes first.

4. It is on Tuesday this year.

5. Mom likes Valentine's Day best.

6. March is my favorite month.

7. We like to go swimming in July.

8. When is President's Day?

9. School starts after Labor Day.

10. My party is on October 1.

**B.** Write each sentence. Use capitals correctly.

11. I really like independence day.

12. The holiday is on the fourth of july.

13. The town parade is on saturday.

14. We have a picnic on sunday.

15. Is there a holiday in august?

## Extra Practice

# Using Capital Letters

**A.** Write each underlined proper noun correctly.

1. My name is <u>greg allen</u>.

2. My family lives in <u>derry</u>.

3. Our house is on <u>oak road</u>.

4. My friend <u>jake</u> has a horse.

5. His horse, <u>patches</u>, is beautiful.

6. I go horseback riding every <u>saturday</u>.

7. The stable is in <u>greenville</u>.

8. I go to riding camp in <u>june</u>.

9. Camp starts around <u>father's day</u>.

10. Camp ends before <u>independence day</u>.

**B.** Write each sentence. Use capitals correctly.

11. Dad and I drove to ohio.

12. Our friend bill has a farm.

13. He sold his horse flash.

14. We drove home on labor day.

15. School starts in september.

# Plural Nouns

**A. Write the underlined word that names more than one.**

1. My <u>sister</u> likes <u>peaches</u>.

2. My <u>brothers</u> share an <u>orange</u>.

3. Who wants a <u>bag</u> of <u>peanuts</u>?

4. I want some <u>pears</u> for <u>lunch</u>.

5. My <u>friend</u> only eats <u>bananas</u>.

6. I have a <u>box</u> of <u>raisins</u>.

7. Are these <u>apples</u> for a <u>pie</u>?

8. Here is a <u>bowl</u> of <u>plums</u>.

9. Put the <u>pits</u> on your <u>plate</u>.

10. Who has the <u>basket</u> of <u>cherries</u>?

**B. Write each sentence. Make the noun in ( ) name more than one.**

11. Look at the (row) of grapes.

12. We need many (bunch).

13. Dad picks ten (box).

14. How many (jar) do we need?

15. Mom makes two jellies and three (jam).

## Extra Practice

# More Plural Nouns

**A.** Write each sentence. Circle the noun that names more than one.

1. All the children have a chore.

2. I feed the ponies.

3. What big teeth they have!

4. My brother likes the bunnies best.

5. Ann feeds the hen and the geese.

6. A baby chick hops around her feet.

7. Our barn cat chases mice.

8. Mom and her friend pick berries.

9. The women will make jam.

10. Two men help Dad with the fence.

**B.** Change the underlined noun from singular to plural. Then write the new sentence.

11. The <u>mouse</u> hid in the barn.

12. The <u>child</u> weeded the garden.

13. The <u>cherry</u> tasted sweet.

14. Our <u>puppy</u> grew quickly.

15. His <u>tooth</u> grew strong.

# Singular Possessive Nouns

**A.** **Write the possessive of each singular noun.**

**1.** Miss Hart

**2.** Toby

**3.** owl

**4.** Max

**5.** Mom

**6.** Ed

**7.** Lee

**8.** Mr. Romano

**9.** woman

**10.** Dina

**B.** **Write each sentence. Use the possessive of the word in ( ).**

**11.** (Everyone) work is so good.

**12.** This (artist) painting is pretty.

**13.** Will (Ryan) drawing win?

**14.** The (winner) name is Carl.

**15.** (Carl) painting wins first prize.

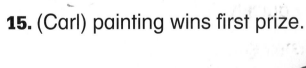

## Extra Practice

# Plural Possessive Nouns

**A.** Write the plural possessive noun in each sentence.

1. My sisters' toys are in the hall.

2. The cats' bowls are in the kitchen.

3. The teachers' meeting starts after lunch.

4. The parents' cars are parked outside.

5. My grandmothers' cookies are the best.

6. The children's pictures hang in the hall.

7. My aunts' store is in the next town.

8. Your friends' fishing trip sounds like fun.

9. We will spend Thanksgiving at our cousins' house.

10. Many people are invited to the two families' party.

**B.** Change each noun in ( ) to a plural possessive noun. Then write each sentence.

11. Welcome to our (family's) picnic.

12. My (sisters) friends are here.

13. Try my (aunts) tasty dishes.

14. Meet my (uncles) children.

15. Are these your (dogs) toys?

# Letter Punctuation

**A.** Write each greeting and closing. Add commas where they belong.

1. Your cousin

2. Dear Grandma

3. With thanks

4. Very truly yours

5. Dear Uncle Ed

6. Sincerely

7. Your grandson

8. Dear Jeff

9. Love to all

10. Dear Mom and Dad

**B.** Write each greeting and closing. Add the correct punctuation.

11. Dear Aunt Bea

12. Very sincerely

13. Dear Alex

14. Love

15. Dear Cousin Ken

## REVIEW THE RULES

- A **subject** and **verb** must agree. Add **-s** or **-es** only if the verb tells about one person or thing.

## More Practice

**A.** Choose the correct verb in ( ). Then write each sentence correctly.

6. Mr. Hall (teach, teaches) cooking.

7. Dan and I (stand, stands) in the kitchen.

8. We (ask, asks) some questions.

9. Mr. Hall (show, shows) us the pots and pans.

10. The cooks (wash, washes) their hands.

**Handbook**
**page 439**

**B.** Spiral Review Write each sentence. Add apostrophes in three possessive nouns. Circle each subject.

11. Amber and I meet a painter.

12. The womans paintings are pretty.

13. We learn many things.

14. The painters brushes stand in a jar.

15. Some brushes tips come to a point.

Extra
Practice
page 198

**Writing Activity** **A Paragraph**

Write about a job in which workers help others.
**APPLY GRAMMAR:** Circle each verb.

Social Studies Link

# Abbreviations

> **RULES**
>
> An **abbreviation** is a short way of writing a word. Abbreviations start with a capital letter and end with a period.
>
> **Will Mr. and Mrs. Sanchez visit the school?**

**Handbook**
pages 447

**Extra Practice**
page 199

## Practice

**A.** Tell how to correct the abbreviation in each sentence.

1. First, ms Dara made paper birds.

2. Next, mr Ling painted pictures.

3. Then dr Fish showed a video.

4. Mark Ross, jr, sang a song.

5. After that, mrs Jones told a story.

**B.** Spiral Review Write each sentence. Make the ending of the verb in ( ) go with the subject. Capitalize each proper noun.

6. Mom, dad, and I (get) ready.

7. Mom (drive) us to jefferson school.

8. Ms. dowd (greet) everyone.

9. Mr. cruz (help) the actors.

10. My friend ali (act) in the play.

**THINK AND WRITE**

**Verbs**

Why do you think there are abbreviations for people's titles? Write your answer.

# Verbs

## REVIEW THE RULES

- An **action verb** is a word that shows action.

- **Present-tense verbs** tell about actions that happen now.

- Add *-s* or *-es* to a present-tense verb only if it tells about one person or thing.

- The **subject** and the **verb** in a sentence need to agree, or go with each other correctly.

- An **abbreviation** is a short way of writing a word.

**Handbook**
page 438

## Practice

**A.** **Write each sentence. Circle the action verb.**

1. James reaches for the telephone.

2. He presses the numbers.

3. Kara's telephone rings.

4. Kara answers the telephone.

5. The two friends make some plans.

**B.** **Challenge** **Write the sentences. Fix any verbs that do not go with the subject. Fix any abbreviations that are not correct.**

**6.–10.** Dr Lee is my uncle. His name is Dave Lee, jr He come to see us. I runs to him. He call me Mr. Mighty.

**Verbs**
Does it help your writing to know about verbs? How?

147

# Past-Tense Verbs

## RULES

**Past-tense verbs** tell about actions that happened before now. To tell about actions in the past, add the ending **-ed** to most verbs.

**Last week we** visited **the zoo.**

If the verb ends in a single consonant, double the consonant and add **-ed.**

If the verb ends in silent **e,** drop the **e** and add **-ed.**

**Mac** dropped **his pencil.**

*drop + p + ed = dropped*

**You** traced **a picture.**

*trace - e + ed = traced*

---

**THINK AND WRITE**

**Verbs**

What helps you remember how to write past-tense verbs correctly?

---

## Guided Practice

**Tell which verb in ( ) shows action in the past.**

1. We (plan, planned) a letter.

2. Jill (opened, opens) her letter.

3. Dot (finished, finishes) her letter.

4. I (pick, picked) up my letter. I folded it.

5. Dan (mailed, mails) the letter.

---
## REVIEW THE RULES

- **Past-tense verbs** tell about actions in the past. Most past-tense verbs end with **-ed: jumped.**

- For verbs like **hop**, double the final consonant before adding **-ed: hopped.** For verbs like **race**, drop the **e** before adding **-ed: raced.**

---

## More Practice

**A. Choose the verb in ( ) that shows action in the past. Then write each sentence.**

**6.** Lisa (stop, stopped) at my desk.

**7.** She (hand, handed) me a letter.

**8.** I (placed, place) the letter in my backpack.

**9.** Some milk (spill, spilled) on the letter.

**10.** I (wipe, wiped) off the milk.

**Handbook**
**page 438**

**Extra Practice**
**page 200**

**B.** Spiral Review **Write each sentence. Underline the action verb. Circle the plural noun.**

**11.** The boys checked their mailbox.

**12.** Luis hoped for a birthday card.

**13.** Letters filled the mailbox.

**14.** The neighbors stopped by.

**15.** Mr. and Mrs. Cliff helped the children.

**Writing Activity   A Self-Portrait**

Write a self-portrait to tell what you did yesterday.
**APPLY GRAMMAR:** Use past-tense verbs and circle them.

149

# The Verb *Have*

**RULES**

The verb *have* has three forms: have, has, and had. *Has* and *have* tell about present actions.

> **Today I** have **a bike. Lin** has **one, too.**

*Had* tells about the past.

> **Yesterday I** had **a scooter.**

See which form of the verb *have* goes with certain subjects. Look at the chart.

| Who or What | Present | Past |
|---|---|---|
| I or you | have | had |
| one person or thing | has | had |
| more than one person or thing | have | had |

## Guided Practice

**Choose the correct verb in ( ).**

1. The museum (has, have) dinosaur bones.

2. You (has, have) a ticket to go in.

3. I (has, have) a ticket, too.

4. Some dinosaurs (has, had) big teeth.

5. Some dinosaurs (have, had) long necks.

## REVIEW THE RULES

Use *have* and *has* for the present tense. Use *had* for the past.

## More Practice

**A. Choose the correct verb in ( ). Write the sentences.**

6. Adam and Nina (have, has) toy dinosaurs.

7. Nina's dinosaur (have, has) a collar.

8. I (have, has) a book about dinosaurs.

9. Some dinosaurs (have, had) big heads.

10. The Apatosaurus (has, had) a small head.

**B. Spiral Review Write each sentence. Write the verb in ( ) to show action in the past. Circle each singular noun.**

11. Yesterday Mom (hand) us a box.

12. My brother (lift) the lid.

13. He and I (pick) up two dinosaurs.

14. We (hug) our mother.

15. She (smile) and kissed us.

**Handbook**
page 440

**Extra Practice**
page 201

### Writing Activity Journal Entry

Write about a favorite toy. Use exact words.
**APPLY GRAMMAR:** Use the verbs *have, has,* and *had* in your journal entry.

151

# Combining Sentences: Verbs

## RULES

Sometimes the subjects of two sentences are the same. You can use *and* to combine the sentences so you do not repeat words.

**Ty swings the bat. Ty hits the ball.**
**Ty swings the bat** and **hits the ball.**

Find subjects that are the same. Combine the predicates with *and*.

<u>Our class</u> *plays kickball.*

↑      ↑
*same*    *combine with* ***and***
↓      ↓

<u>Our class</u> *wins games.*

**Our class** *plays kickball and wins games.*

**THINK AND WRITE**

**Verbs**

Why would you combine two short sentences with *and* in your writing? Write your answer.

## Guided Practice

**Use *and* to combine the underlined predicates. Write the new sentence.**

**1.** Sue <u>sees the ball</u>. Sue <u>hits it</u>.

**2.** The ball <u>flies</u>. The ball <u>falls</u>.

**3.** Drew <u>gets the ball</u>. Drew <u>throws it</u>.

**4.** Sue <u>runs to the base</u>. Sue <u>slides</u>.

**5.** Al <u>grabs the ball</u>. Al <u>tags Sue</u>.

# Mechanics and Spelling

## Directions

Read the passage and decide which type of mistake appears in each underlined section. Choose the correct answer.

---

**Sample**

On June 21 2000, Olga rode her bike to the
<u>(1)</u>
pet store. Inside <u>she saw hamsters runing</u> in
<u>(2)</u>
circles on a wheel. She saw lizards crawling

up a stick. She saw snakes curled up in knots.

Then she saw a green and blue parrot that

said, "I see you." <u>That made olga laugh</u>.
<u>(3)</u>

*Check to see if commas are needed in the date.*

*Do you have to double the consonant before adding the ending?*

*Every proper noun begins with a capital letter.*

---

**1** ○ Spelling
   ○ Capitalization
   ○ Punctuation

**2** ○ Spelling
   ○ Capitalization
   ○ Punctuation

**3** ○ Spelling
   ○ Capitalization
   ○ Punctuation

**Test Tip**
If you don't understand something, read it again carefully.

157

# TIME FOR KIDS Writer's Notebook

**RESEARCH** If I want to find out where a place is, I look at a **map**. Maps help me find cities, towns, mountains, lakes, rivers, and oceans. Sometimes I put a map in my story. Maps show my readers where a place is.

**RESEARCH**

**WRITING WELL** When I write a story, I always start at the beginning. Then I tell what happened **in order**. Writing events in order helps readers follow my story.

**COMPOSITION SKILLS**

**USING WORDS** Adding a few letters before a word can change its meaning. Those letters are called a **prefix**. Prefixes can help me change the <u>usual</u> into the <u>unusual</u>. Using these words can help me say exactly what I want to say. Can you think of any words with prefixes?

**VOCABULARY SKILLS**

## Read Now!

As you read the photo essay about the friendly firehouse, write down words or phrases that tell about the order of events in the essay.

158

# TIME
## FOR KIDS
### PHOTO ESSAY

FIRE DEPARTMENT

# A Very Friendly Firehouse

Firefighters jump at the idea
of having fun with kids.

# Firefighters Keep Kids in School

"Good Morning!" A firefighter says hello to a group of kids from the neighborhood.

The firefighters of Engine Company 16 battle fires in Chicago, Illinois. But when they aren't fighting fires, they do something very unusual. They open their firehouse doors to kids.

The story begins about 15 years ago. Back then, children from Hartigan Elementary School were not going to class. Instead, they were visiting the firehouse during school hours.

So firefighter Arthur Lewis had an idea. Kids who started going to school would win a radio. Later, the men gave away old bikes which they rebuilt. The idea worked. Kids stayed in school!

Today, all kinds of stuff goes on at the firehouse. Kids play sports and chess. Kids practice math.

Jeremy Woods drops by the firehouse to play football. "It's my favorite place to come," he says.

interNET CONNECTION Go to www.mhschool.com/language-arts for more information on the topic.

# Vocabulary and Comprehension

## Directions

Read the paragraph. Then read each question that follows the paragraph. Choose the best answer to each question.

---

**Sample**

Are you getting a new puppy? Here's how to get ready for it. First, get a box and some old sweaters to make a soft, warm bed. Next, fill a bowl with water and another bowl with food. Be sure to <u>unfold</u> some newspapers and spread them all around. Then, get a collar and leash ready. Finally, you will be able to run and play with your new dog.

---

*Look for small word parts to help figure out the word's meaning.*

**1** What is the first thing you need to do to get ready for a puppy?

○ Get a collar and leash.

○ Think of a name.

○ Make a soft, warm bed.

**2** In this paragraph, the word <u>unfold</u> means—

○ read

○ make not folded

○ make not full

# Seeing Like a Writer

Look at these pictures. How would you explain what the people are doing? What words would you use to describe each step?

***Hayley and Her Violin*** by Patricia Espir.

## Writing from Pictures

1. Think about what actions the pictures show. Write three action words for the pictures.

2. Write a caption for one of the pictures. Tell what the children are doing and how to do it.

3. Choose two of the pictures. Write a paragraph telling what the pictures show.

**Apply Grammar:** Include present-tense verbs that add -*s* or -*es*. Circle each one.

# Explanatory Writing

Think about a time when you tried to teach someone how to do something. Explanatory writing is like that. It goes step by step.

## Learning from Writers

Read these pieces of explanatory writing.

**THINK AND WRITE**

**Purpose**
How can you write directions that are easy to understand? Write your answer.

## The Marching Band

Bobby watched the boys and girls on his street march back and forth. Each one played a different instrument. If Bobby had an instrument, he could be in the band, too. Bobby was lucky. His grandma showed him how to make a humming horn.

First, Bobby cut a four-by-four-inch square of waxed paper. Next, he placed the paper over one end of an empty paper tube. He used a rubber band to hold the paper in place. Last, Bobby's Grandma used a sharp pencil to poke holes through the tube.

To play his horn, Bobby held the tube next to his mouth and hummed. He moved his fingers to cover and uncover the holes. Soon, Bobby was humming along with the rest of the band!

— Dale Ryder

## My Peanut Butter and Jelly Sandwich

Do you want to know what my favorite lunch in the world is? It's a peanut butter and jelly sandwich and a glass of milk! Here's how to make your own.

First, you get two pieces of bread. Next, you get the peanut butter and jelly. Open them up and put them near the bread. Get a butter knife and smush the peanut butter onto one piece of bread. Then, smush the jelly onto the other piece. Smush both pieces together and you have a peanut butter and jelly sandwich. It's delicious!

— Ken Lee

## PRACTICE and APPLY

**Thinking Like a Reader**

1. How did Bobby make the horn?

2. What step comes after putting the peanut butter on the bread?

**Thinking Like a Writer**

3. Why did Dale Ryder name all the materials for making a horn?

4. What space-order words did Ken Lee use?

5. **Reading Across Texts** Tell how the two explanations are alike. How are they different?

# Features of Explanatory Writing

---
## DEFINITIONS AND FEATURES
---

**Explanatory writing** tells how to do something. Good explanatory writing does these things:

▶ It tells **how to** complete a task.

▶ It gives **step-by-step** instructions.

▶ It uses **time-order** or **space-order words**.

## ▶ How-To

Reread "The Marching Band" on page 172. What does this story explain how to make?

> Bobby was lucky. His grandma showed him how to make a humming horn.

The author tells how Bobby makes the horn. The instructions teach the reader how, too.

## ▶ Step-by-Step Instructions

The directions in the story go step by step. The first step has to be completed before going on to the next step.

> First, Bobby cut a four-by-four-inch square of waxed paper. Next, he placed the paper over one end of an empty paper tube.

▶ **Space-Order Words**

Space-order words add important details to directions. Use words like on, over, under, and near when you write about how to do something.

> To play his humming horn, Bobby held the tube next to his mouth and hummed.

What space-order words did the author use to help the reader understand how to make a humming horn?

| Features | Examples |
| --- | --- |
|  |  |

**PRACTICE and APPLY**

**Create a Features Chart**

1. List the features of explanatory writing.

2. Reread "My Peanut Butter and Jelly Sandwich" on page 173.

3. Write how the author used each feature.

# Prewrite

Explanatory writing explains how to do something. When you give directions, you are writing to explain.

## Purpose and Audience

The purpose of explanatory writing is to inform. Think of who is reading your directions. Decide what he or she needs to know.

## Choose a Topic

Start by **brainstorming** a list of topics. Think of an event coming up at school. Work out the directions for getting there.

**Explore and list ideas** to put in your invitation.

**THINK AND WRITE**

**Audience**
How would your invitation be different if you wrote it to someone in your family. Write your answer.

*I have lots of ideas for my letter.*

Invite Dr. Jones to pet show

Pet show at school on December 17

My dog Rex has brown fur.

Go to the office.

Sign in.

Go through the doors.

Go down the hall.

Go up the stairs.

Turn.

## Organize • Sequence

Your invitation will give directions to the event. To plan the order of your directions, use a list-of-steps chart.

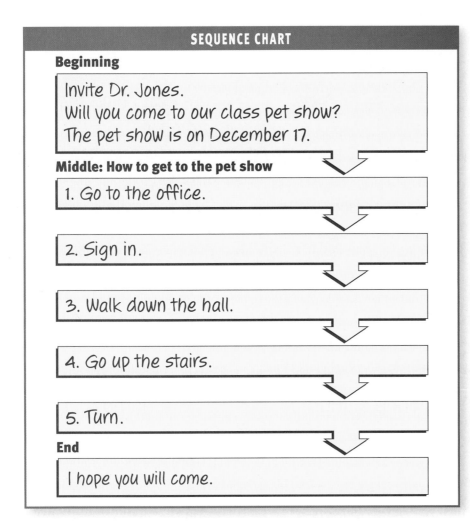

**SEQUENCE CHART**

**Beginning**

Invite Dr. Jones.
Will you come to our class pet show?
The pet show is on December 17.

**Middle: How to get to the pet show**

1. Go to the office.

2. Sign in.

3. Walk down the hall.

4. Go up the stairs.

5. Turn.

**End**

I hope you will come.

## PRACTICE and APPLY

### Plan Your Own Explanatory Writing

1. Choose an event and a person to invite.

2. Brainstorm ideas about the event.

3. Put the steps of the directions in order.

## Checklist ✓

**Prewriting**

- Did you tell when the event takes place?

- Did you think about your purpose and your audience?

- Did you choose a person to invite?

- Have you put the steps of your directions in order?

- Do you need to find out more?

## Prewrite • Research and Inquiry

### ▶ Writer's Resources

You may need to do some research for your invitation. Start with a list of questions. Then find resources that answer them.

| What Else Do I Need to Know? | Where Can I Find the Information? |
|---|---|
| Where does Doctor Jones live? | Look in the telephone directory. |
| Which classroom do you pass before you go up the stairs? | Check the school map. |

### ▶ Telephone Directory

You can look in a telephone directory to find someone's address or telephone number. The names are listed in ABC order.

*Look for the last name of the person.*

*Use the guide names to help you find the right page.*

| 418 | JONES—JORDAN |
|---|---|

| | | | | | |
|---|---|---|---|---|---|
| Jones Cathy | 22 Washington St | 555-0234 | Jordan David | 155 River Dr | 555-2281 |
| Jones Donna | 40 Morris Rd | 555-1299 | Jordan Dennis | 602 Lincoln Rd | 555-8743 |
| Jones Ellen | 33 West Ave | 555-6624 | Jordan Ed | 29 Garden Rd | 555-9876 |
| Jones Larry | 495 River Dr | 555-7543 | Jordan Maria | 700 Cove Pl | 555-2901 |
| Jones Dr. Lisa | 37 Garden Rd | 555-4675 | Jordan Paul | 221 River Dr | 555-3417 |

*Look for the first name of the person.*

## ▶ A Map

A map can help as you write your directions. Include places to look for, so readers can be sure they are going in the right direction.

## ▶ Use Your Research

Now that you have done your research, you can use it in your invitation. Add details from your research to your chart.

**Handbook**
pages 458–459

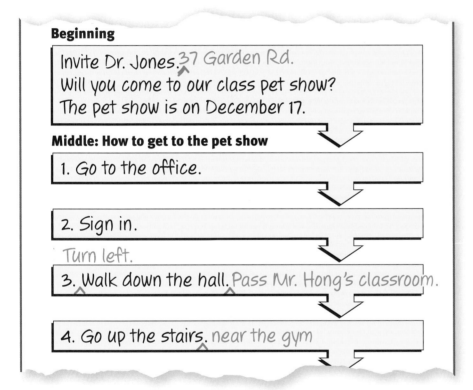

**Beginning**

Invite Dr. Jones. 37 Garden Rd.
Will you come to our class pet show?
The pet show is on December 17.

**Middle: How to get to the pet show**

1. Go to the office.

2. Sign in.
   Turn left.

3. Walk down the hall. Pass Mr. Hong's classroom.

4. Go up the stairs. near the gym

## Checklist ✓

**Research and Inquiry**

- Did you make a list of questions?

- Did you use resources to answer your questions?

- Did you add your answers to your chart?

## PRACTICE and APPLY
### Review Your Plan

1. List questions you have about your letter.

2. Use resources to answer your questions.

3. Add new information to your chart.

# Draft

Before you write your draft, look over your list of steps. Be sure they are in the right order. You want your audience to be able to follow your directions easily.

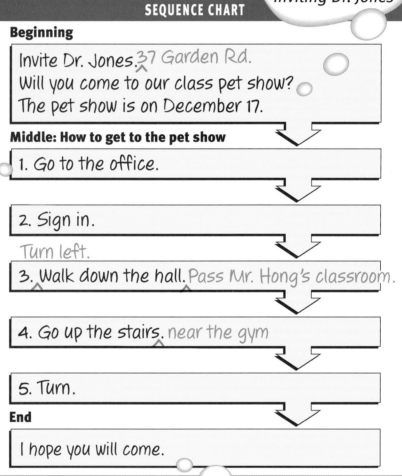

*Main idea for first paragraph: Inviting Dr. Jones*

**SEQUENCE CHART**

**Beginning**

Invite Dr. Jones. 37 Garden Rd.
Will you come to our class pet show?
The pet show is on December 17.

**Middle: How to get to the pet show**

1. Go to the office.

2. Sign in.

Turn left.
3. Walk down the hall. Pass Mr. Hong's classroom.

4. Go up the stairs. near the gym

5. Turn.

**End**

I hope you will come.

*Main idea for second paragraph: Directions to the pet show*

*This will be a good way to end the letter.*

**Writing PROCESS**

✓ **Checklist**

**Drafting**

- Did you think about your purpose and your audience?

- Does your letter tell how to get to the event?

- Does the order of the steps make sense?

- Did you use words that make your directions easy to follow?

Look at this draft. The writer used ideas from her chart and added some details.

PREWRITE

DRAFT

REVISE

PROOFREAD

PUBLISH

**DRAFT**

37 Garden Rd.

Lincoln Illinois 60646 ........................................ Heading

Dear Dr Jones ........................................ Greeting

You are my dog's doctor. Will you come to our class pet show? It is December 17. ........................................ The first paragraph tells about the pet show.

Here is how to get to the pet show. Go to the office. Sign in. Then turn left. Walk past Mr. Hong's classroom. Finally, go up the stairs near the gym and turn. I hopes you can come. Please let me know. ........................................ Body

........................................ The second paragraph gives directions to the pet show.

Amy Wong ........................................ Signature

## PRACTICE and APPLY
### Draft Your Own Explanatory Writing

1. Look back at your chart.

2. Use words that will make the steps clearer.

3. Use a map to help you give directions.

**TIP!**

TECHNOLOGY

**Highlight parts of your letter that you might want to move. Then use the cut or paste features.**

# Revise

### Elaborate

In your letter, you can elaborate by adding details to your directions. This writer added important details.

> It is December 17. It starts at 1:30.
> ^

> Sign in. at the desk
> ^

## SPACE-ORDER WORDS

| | |
|---|---|
| behind | near |
| below | next to |
| beside | north |
| by | opposite |
| east | right |
| in front | south |
| left | west |

### Word Choice

Space-order words help readers follow directions. Look at the word this writer added to her draft. Which words tell about where places are?

> Finally, go up the stairs near the gym and turn. right
> ^

### Conferencing for the Reader

■ Check to see if your partner's writing
- gives step-by-step instructions
- uses time-order words
- uses space-order words

# Better Paragraphs

Think about the main ideas you want to tell. Each main idea should be its own paragraph.

PREWRITE

DRAFT

REVISE

PROOFREAD

PUBLISH

## REVISE

37 Garden Rd.

Lincoln Illinois 60646

Dear Dr Jones

    You are my dog's doctor. Will you come to
our class pet show? It is December 17. *It starts at 1:30.*

    Here is how to get to the pet show. *First,* Go to
the office. Sign in *at the desk*. Then turn left. Walk past
Mr. Hong's classroom. Finally, go up the stairs
near the gym and turn *right*. I hopes you can

come. Please let me know.

Amy Wong

## Checklist ✓
### Revising

- Did you keep your purpose and your audience in mind?

- Do you need more details?

- Are the steps in the directions clear?

- Do you have different kinds of sentences?

## PRACTICE and APPLY
### Revise Your Own Explanatory Writing

1. Read your draft to yourself.

2. Share your draft with a partner.

3. Add details to make your directions easier.

4. **Grammar** Do your subjects and verbs agree?

## Writing PROCESS

# Proofread

After you revise your letter, go back and read it again. Look for a different kind of mistake.

> ### STRATEGIES FOR PROOFREADING
>
> - **Look for names of people, places, months, and holidays.** Start each with a capital letter.
>
> - **Check for punctuation.** Make sure you added commas after the greeting, closing, between the city and state, and between the day and year.
>
> - **Check your spelling.** Use a dictionary.

### TiP!

**TECHNOLOGY**

**When you work on a computer, a spell checker program can help you find words that are spelled wrong. Check that the new spelling matches the word you want to write.**

## REVIEW THE RULES

**GRAMMAR**

- A **present-tense verb** must match the subject of the sentence. Add **-s** to present-tense verbs that tell about one person or thing.

- Add **-ed** to **past-tense action verbs** that tell about the past.

**MECHANICS**

- Start **abbreviations** in people's titles with a capital letter and end with a period.

- In a **date**, write a comma between the day and the year.

**STEP 2**

# How to Show Your Invitation
## Suggestions for Illustrations

Show pictures or maps to help your audience.

- Make a poster. List important facts, such as dates and times.
- Show a map of the directions.
- Make your pictures, maps, or posters big enough so people can see them easily.

**STEP 3**

# How to Share Your Invitation
## Strategies for Rehearsing  If you practice ahead of time, you'll be ready.

- Find a quiet place to practice.
- Ask a partner or family member to listen to you and give you ideas.

**TiP!**

### Viewing Strategies

- Read the information shown on posters or pictures.

- Make sure you understand maps and diagrams.

- Take notes about important facts and directions.

## PRACTICE and APPLY

### Rehearse Your Invitation

1. Get your note cards together.

2. Find or make the pictures you will use.

3. Practice saying your invitation out loud.

4. Smile and sound interested when you speak.

# Writing Tests

Remember to read the prompt carefully. Look for key words and phrases that tell you what to write about and how to do your writing.

*Look for words that tell if the purpose is to entertain or inform.*

*What words tell who the audience is?*

*Look for words that tell what kind of writing this is.*

> **Prompt**
>
> **Think of a special activity that you know <u>how to do.</u>**
>
> **Write a paragraph <u>for your teacher</u> that tells <u>what you can do and how you do it.</u> Be sure to use details to tell about it.**

## How to Read a Prompt

**Purpose**  Look for words in the prompt that tell you the purpose of the writing. The words "how to do" tell you that the purpose will be to inform. When you explain how to do something, you give the audience information.

**Audience**  The prompt tells who the audience is. The words "for your teacher" let you know that your teacher is the audience.

**Explanatory Writing**  In explanatory writing, you tell how to do something. The words "what you can do and how you do it" let you know that you should explain what to do step-by-step.

**Test Tip**
Remember to take your time and do your work carefully.

**Same or Different** When you see something flying high up in the sky, how can you tell if it's a bird or a plane? How are birds and planes alike and how are they different?

Write an article that compares birds and planes. Include exact details and put them in an order that makes sense.

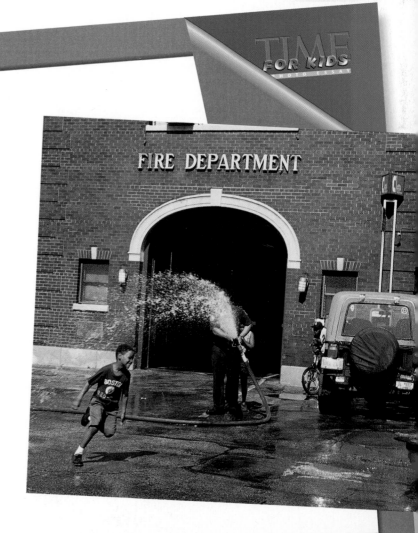

TIME FOR KIDS

PROJECT 2

# Directions

Has a firefighter ever talked to you and your classmates about what to do if there is a fire in your home or school?

**What to Do in Case of a FIRE** Write a set of directions that tells how to get out of your home or school in case of a fire.

## Extra Practice

# Action Verbs

**A.** Write the sentences. Write each underlined word that is an action verb.

1. My friends <u>walk</u> <u>to</u> my house.

2. <u>First</u>, we <u>eat</u> lunch.

3. Mel and Tom <u>ride</u> their <u>bikes</u>.

4. Greg <u>skates</u> in the <u>driveway</u>.

5. Jack and Dad <u>shoot</u> <u>baskets</u>.

6. Lori <u>and</u> I <u>play</u> jump rope.

7. Mom <u>holds</u> the <u>rope</u>.

8. <u>All</u> my friends <u>clap</u>.

9. Dad <u>cheers</u> <u>for</u> Mom.

10. <u>Dad</u> <u>jumps</u> high, too.

**B.** Write each sentence. Circle each action verb.

11. Jack and I wave to our friends.

12. We race to the playground.

13. Mel and Tom run together.

14. Terry skips rope by herself.

15. Luis runs the fastest.

# Present-Tense Verbs

**A.** **Choose the correct word in ( ). Then write each sentence.**

1. My friend (watch, watches) the softball team.

2. Jan (pitch, pitches) for the team.

3. Jan's twin sister (catch, catches) for the team.

4. Ann (buy, buys) a new mitt.

5. The new mitt (fit, fits) Ann's hand.

6. Jan's sister (save, saves) her money.

7. Mrs. Jones (coach, coaches) the girls.

8. The girl's brother (help, helps), too.

9. The team (play, plays) on Saturday mornings.

10. Each player (practice, practices) for the game.

**B.** **Add *-s* or *-es* to the verb in ( ). Then write each sentence.**

11. The big game (begin) soon.

12. Each girl (get) ready.

13. Ann (drink) a cup of water before the game.

14. Jan (stretch) her arms and legs.

15. The coach (wish) everyone luck.

197

## Extra Practice

# Subject-Verb Agreement

**A.** Choose the correct form of the verb in ( ).
Then write each sentence.

1. Many people (work, works) in my neighborhood.

2. Miss Simms (deliver, delivers) our mail.

3. We (buy, buys) bread from Mrs. Barton.

4. Ben and Diane (mow, mows) lawns.

5. Mom and Dad (teach, teaches) school.

6. Officer Jones ( keep, keeps) us safe.

7. Mr. Sung and Mr. Yin (fix, fixes) cars.

8. Uncle Bob (fight, fights) fires.

9. My sister and I (help, helps) our neighbors.

10. Dr. Ruiz (check, checks) our teeth.

**B.** Write the sentence. Change the verb in ( )
to show action going on now.

11. Dad (need) wood and paint.

12. We (drive) to the store.

13. Mr. Lee (own) the store.

14. Mr. Lee, Dad, and I (load) the truck.

15. Now Dad (finish) painting the bookcase.

**D. Write the words in a series in each sentence.**

**16.** Sara, Max, and I go riding.

**17.** Blaze, Red, and Star are our horses.

**18.** Star's tail, mane, and ears are black.

**19.** The horses eat oats, bran, and hay.

**20.** Where are my boots, saddle, and helmet?

## Unit 2 Nouns

**A. Write the noun in each sentence. Write if it names a person, place, or thing. Write if it is singular or plural.**

**21.** The children are hungry.

**22.** Who wants sandwiches?

**23.** Come out to the kitchen.

**24.** Will you call your father?

**25.** Get the glasses, please.

**B. Write the proper nouns in each sentence correctly.**

**26.** Last monday was independence day.

**27.** I spent the fourth of july in philadelphia.

**28.** We watched the parade on market street.

**29.** Aunt paula took greg and me.

**30.** Her dog sparky barked at the fireworks.

## Cumulative Review

**C. Write the possessive form of each noun.**

**31.** girls

**32.** teacher

**33.** nurses

**34.** family

**35.** friends

**D. Punctuate each greeting or closing.**

**36.** Dear Uncle Bob

**37.** With my thanks

**38.** Dear Grandpa

**39.** Your best friend

**40.** Dear Dad

### Unit 3 Verbs

**A. Write each sentence. Use the correct verb in ( ).**

**41.** I (brush, brushes) my teeth after meals.

**42.** Ted and Ben (floss, flosses) at night.

**43.** Our mom (fix, fixes) healthful meals.

**44.** Ted, Ben, and I (visit, visits) the dentist.

**45.** The dentist (check, checks) our teeth.

**B.** Change the underlined verb in each sentence to the past tense. Write the new sentence.

**46.** Mom <u>has</u> a birthday.

**47.** Dan and I <u>wrap</u> her gifts.

**48.** Dad <u>helps</u> us.

**49.** Mom <u>likes</u> our gifts.

**50.** She <u>hugs</u> both of us.

**C.** Combine the pairs of sentences. Underline each verb in your new sentences.

**51.** Dad grabbed his banjo. Dad played.

**52.** Mom stood up. Mom sang.

**53.** We sat in a circle. We listened.

**54.** Sara clapped. Sara danced.

**55.** Everyone laughed. Everyone cheered.

**D.** Write each date correctly.

**56.** July 4 1776

**57.** January 1 2000

**58.** April 9 1865

**59.** May 5 1961

**60.** October 12 1492

208

# Verbs and Writing That Compares

In this unit you will learn more about verbs. You will also learn how to compare things in your writing.

**Science Link** Birds and bats both fly, but they are not the same. See what makes them different.

Bats are also good hunters because they are expert fliers. Their wings are different from bird wings. Bat wings have long arm bones with extra-long finger bones. A thin skin called a membrane stretches between the bones. The membrane connects the wing bones to the bat's legs and body.

from *Zipping, Zapping, Zooming Bats* by Ann Earle

## Thinking Like a Writer

**Writing That Compares**
Writing that compares tells about two things, places, people, or ideas.

• How are bats different from birds?

**Verbs** The author uses forms of the verb *be*, such as *am, is,* or *are.*

**QUICK WRITE** Find a sentence with <u>am</u>, <u>is</u>, or <u>are</u>. Write another sentence using that word.

# The Verb *Be*

## RULES

The verb *be* has special forms in the present tense and in the past tense.

| Subject | Present | Past |
|---|---|---|
| I | am | was |
| she, he, it | is | was |
| you, we, they | are | were |

*Am, is,* and *are* tell about the present time. *Was* and *were* tell about the past.

| Present Time | Past Time |
|---|---|
| I am here. | I was here yesterday. |
| She is here. | She was here yesterday. |
| We are here today. | We were here yesterday. |

## THINK AND WRITE

### Verbs

How do you know if a sentence is about the present time or the past? Write your answer.

## Guided Practice

**Choose the correct form of the verb *be* in ( ).**

**1.** Last night the sky (is, was) cloudy.

**2.** We (was, were) inside.

**3.** Tonight the stars (are, were) bright.

**4.** The moon (is, are) full.

**5.** Now I (am, was) not sleepy.

---

**REVIEW THE RULES**

- The verb *be* has special forms in the present tense (*am, is, are*) and in the past tense (*was, were*).

---

## More Practice

**A.** **Choose the correct form of the verb *be* in ( ). Write the sentence correctly.**

6. Last night (is, was) very cold.

7. This morning the snow (is, are) deep.

8. Now I (am, was) ready to go outside.

9. Yesterday the streets (are, were) bare.

10. Today the streets (are, am) snowy.

**B.** Spiral Review **Write each sentence. Circle each word that is a form of the verb *be*. Underline each action verb.**

11. Yesterday the snow was soft.

12. The snowdrifts were very high.

13. Today the snow is sticky.

14. We roll three big snowballs.

15. We make a wonderful snowman!

**Handbook**
**page 440**

**Extra Practice**
**page 268**

### Writing Activity A Paragraph

Write a paragraph about something that is happening now or that happened yesterday.
**APPLY GRAMMAR:** Circle forms of the verb *be*.

# Helping Verbs

## RULES

A **helping verb** helps another verb to show an action. The verbs *be* and *have* can be helping verbs.

Use forms of *be* to tell about things that are happening now.

**We** <u>are</u> **planning** a picnic.
↑ ↑
*helping verb   verb*

Use forms of *have* to tell about things that have already happened.

**We** <u>have</u> **planned** a picnic.
↑ ↑
*helping verb   verb*

**THiNK AND WRITE**

**Verbs**

How does a helping verb help another verb? Write your answer.

## Guided Practice

**Name the helping verb in each sentence.**

**1.** We are playing on the beach.

**2.** We have played here many times before.

**3.** I am swimming in the ocean.

**4.** Aunt Kathy is wading nearby.

**5.** Ben has built a sand castle.

- A **helping verb** helps tell about an action.

- *Am, is,* and *are* can help tell about action that is happening now.

- *Has* and *have* can help tell about things that already happened.

## More Practice

**A. Write each sentence. Circle the helping verb.**

**6.** We have brought a picnic lunch.

**7.** Dad is giving out the sandwiches.

**8.** Mom has fixed the beach umbrella.

**9.** We are sitting in the shade.

**10.** Let's play after we have rested.

**Handbook**
**page 441**

**Extra**
**Practice**
**page 269**

**B.** Spiral Review **Write the letter. Correct the greeting and the closing. Fill in each blank with the correct form of *be*.**

**11.–15.** Dear Aunt Kathy

How ____ you? Yesterday ____ an exciting day! Today I ____ tired but happy.

Love

Lucy

### Writing Activity   A Journal Entry

Write a journal entry about a special day you had.
**APPLY GRAMMAR:** Circle each helping verb.

213

# Linking Verbs

---
**RULES**
---

A **linking verb** is a verb that does not show action. The verb *be* is a linking verb.

> **We are happy.**
> **Our dog is a winner.**

The verb *be* links the subject to words that tell something about the subject.

> **Pixie is proud.   Pixie stands still.**
>
> linking verb              action verb

## THINK AND WRITE

**Verbs**

What makes a linking verb different from other verbs? Write your answer in your journal.

## Guided Practice

**Name the verb in each sentence. Tell if the verb is a linking verb or an action verb.**

**1.** Yesterday's dog show was exciting.

**2.** My dog Pixie is a toy poodle.

**3.** Toy poodles are small dogs.

**4.** I hold Pixie in my arms.

**5.** Everybody pets Pixie.

**REVIEW THE RULES**

- A **linking verb** is a verb that does not show action.

- The verb *be* is a linking verb.

## More Practice

**A.** **Write each sentence. Underline the verb. Then write *linking verb* or *action verb*.**

6. Mr. King's dog is a boxer.

7. Boxers are friendly dogs.

8. Mr. King trained his dog Rusty.

9. Rusty was a smart puppy.

10. Now Rusty works for Mr. King.

**Handbook**
**page 438**

**Extra Practice**
**page 270**

**B.** Spiral Review **Write each sentence. Underline the subject. Circle the helping verb.**

11. Mom and I have enjoyed dog shows.

12. Mom has ordered our tickets.

13. We are going to the show today.

14. I am brushing Major's shiny coat.

15. Major is waiting for a treat.

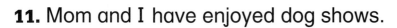

**Writing Activity**   **A Paragraph**

Write about how two pets are alike or different.
**APPLY GRAMMAR:** Circle each linking verb.

**Science Link**

215

# Commas in Names of Places

---
**RULES**

Use a **comma** between the name of a city and a state.

**Wendy lives in Columbus, Ohio.**

---

## Practice

**A. Tell where the comma belongs in each sentence.**

**Extra Practice page 271**

1. The family started in Ames Iowa.

2. They drove to Lincoln Nebraska.

3. Then they went to Topeka Kansas.

4. They stopped in Tulsa Oklahoma.

5. They visited friends in Dallas Texas.

**THINK AND WRITE**

**Commas**

Why do you write a comma between the name of a city and state?

**B.** Spiral Review **Write each sentence. Fix three abbreviations. Underline each action verb. Circle each linking verb.**

6. Mr and Mrs Oak live in Arizona.

7. They work at the Grand Canyon.

8. Mrs Oak is a tour guide.

9. She takes people on mule rides.

10. Mules are strong animals.

216

# Verbs

## REVIEW THE RULES

- The verb *be* has special forms. *Am*, *is*, and *are* tell about now. *Was* and *were* tell about the past.

- A **helping verb** helps another verb show action. *Be* and *have* are helping verbs.

- A **linking verb** does not show action. *Be* links the subject to words that describe it.

- A **comma** separates a city's name and a state's name.

**Handbook**
pages 440–441

## Practice

**A.** Use the correct verb in ( ). Write each sentence.

1. Last week I (was, were) at home.

2. My cousins (was, were) on vacation then.

3. Some mail (is, are) in our mailbox.

4. Now I (am, was) happy.

5. Now two postcards (are, were) on my wall!

**B.** **Challenge** Write *am*, *is*, *are*, *was*, *were*, *have*, or *has* in each sentence.

6.–10. Lora's friend Carlos _____ gone to camp. Lora _____ sad on the day Carlos left. Mom and Dad _____ seen her sad face. Now they _____ planning a surprise for Lora.

**QUICK WRITE**

**Verbs**
Use linking and helping verbs to write three sentences. Use commas correctly.

# The Verbs *Go* and *Do*

## RULES

Some verbs do not add **-ed** in the past tense.

The verbs *go* and *do* have special forms in the past tense. They are called irregular verbs.

The past tense forms of *go* and *do* do not end in *-ed*.

| Verb | Past Tense | Example |
|------|-----------|---------|
| go | went | I went to school |
| do | did | I did my homework |

**THINK AND WRITE**

**Verbs**

How are irregular verbs different from other verbs? Write the answer in your journal.

## Guided Practice

**Change the underlined verb to the tense in ( ). Write the new sentence.**

**1.** I <u>go</u> to the library. (past)

**2.** Eva <u>went</u> with me. (present)

**3.** First we <u>do</u> some reading. (past)

**4.** I <u>do</u> an outline. (past)

**5.** Then Eva <u>did</u> a first draft. (present)

---
**REVIEW THE RULES**

- The past tense of *go* is **went**.

- The past tense of *do* is **did**.
---

## More Practice

**A. Change the underlined verb to the tense shown in ( ). Write the new sentence.**

**6.** Sometimes the rain <u>goes</u> on for days. (past)

**7.** The showers <u>did</u> not stop. (present)

**8.** The soil <u>does</u> not soak up the rain. (past)

**9.** After the rain, the clouds <u>go</u> away. (past)

**10.** The puddles <u>did</u> not dry up. (present)

**B.** Spiral Review **Write each sentence. Underline each action verb. Circle each linking verb.**

**11.** The weather changed quickly.

**12.** Now the sky is dark.

**13.** The clouds are low and gray.

**14.** The wind blows.

**15.** The children run inside.

**Handbook**
**page 441**

**Extra**
**Practice**
**page 272**

---
**Writing Activity** **An Interview**

Write three questions to ask a weather reporter.
**APPLY GRAMMAR:** Use forms of the verbs *go* and *do*.

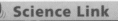

Science Link

---

# The Verbs *Say, See,* and *Run*

## RULES

Irregular verbs do not add **-ed** to form the past tense.

*Say, see,* and *run* are irregular verbs.

The past tense forms of **say**, **see**, and **run** do not end in **-ed**.

| Verb | Past Tense | Example |
|------|------------|---------|
| say | said | We said, "Good luck." |
| see | saw | We saw the runners. |
| run | ran | They ran fast. |

**THINK AND WRITE**

**Verbs**

Write to tell why *say, see,* and *run* are called irregular verbs.

## Guided Practice

**Complete each sentence with the past-tense form of the verb in ( ).**

**1.** My friends _____ the race. (see)

**2.** They _____, "Wow!" (say)

**3.** They _____ so many riders! (see)

**4.** I _____, "I don't like bike races." (say)

**5.** I _____ in a race. (run)

---
**REVIEW** THE **RULES**

- The past tense of *say* is ***said***.

- The past tense of *see* is ***saw***.

- The past tense of *run* is ***ran***.

---

## More Practice

**A.** **Fill in the blank with the past-tense form of the verb in ( ). Write each sentence.**

6. I _____ around the track. (run)

7. I _____ my family cheering for me. (see)

8. Somebody _____, "Here, Snuffy!" (say)

9. I _____ a little dog on the track. (see)

10. It _____ beside me to the finish line. (run)

**B.** Spiral Review **Write the paragraph. Change the present forms of *go* and *be* to past forms. Add commas where needed.**

**11.–15.** We go to the school track for the race. My brother goes to the starting line. Mr. Cho Ms. Mann and Dr. Jay are the judges.

**Handbook**
**page 441**

Extra
Practice
**page 273**

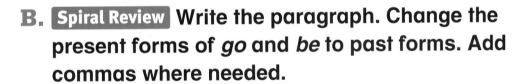

### Writing Activity  Story

Write a story about a race or another sport.
**APPLY GRAMMAR:** Use the past forms of the verbs *say*, *see*, and *run* in your story. Circle the verbs.

# The Verbs *Come, Give,* and *Sing*

---

**RULES**

The past-tense forms of irregular verbs do not end in **-ed**.

*Come, give,* and *sing* are irregular verbs.

The past-tense forms of **come**, **give**, and **sing** do not end in **-ed**.

| Verb | Past Tense | Example |
|------|-----------|---------|
| come | came | She came to the stage. |
| give | gave | She gave everyone smiles. |
| sing | sang | She sang a silly song. |

---

**THINK AND WRITE**

**Verbs**

What is the same about the past-tense forms of *give, come,* and *sing?* Write your answer.

## Guided Practice

**Complete each sentence with the past-tense form of the verb in ( ).**

**1.** We _____ out many invitations. (give)

**2.** Families _____ to the show. (come)

**3.** Some children _____ songs. (sing)

**4.** Our school's principal _____, too. (sing)

**5.** My friend Beth _____ a speech. (give)

## REVIEW THE RULES

- The past tense of *come* is **came**.
- The past tense of *give* is **gave**.
- The past tense of *sing* is **sang**.

## More Practice

**A.** **Complete each sentence with the past form of the verb in ( ). Write each sentence.**

6. Emily _____ a song by herself. (sing)

7. She _____ to the front of the room. (come)

8. She _____ a little bow. (give)

9. Then she _____ very softly. (sing)

10. Everyone _____ her a big cheer. (give)

**Handbook**
**page 441**

**Extra Practice page 274**

**B.** Spiral Review **Use *and* to join each pair of sentences. Write each new sentence in the past tense.**

11. Max goes to school. Max sees his friends.

12. We see our teacher. We run to her.

13. Mrs. Kato smiles. Mrs. Kato says hello.

14. Tyler sees a bird. Tyler sings to it.

15. Alexa waves. Alexa runs over.

**Writing Activity** **A Poster**

Make a poster about a school show.
**APPLY GRAMMAR:** Use and circle the verbs *come*, *give*, and *sing* in your poster.

Art Link

223

# Contractions with *not*

## RULES

A **contraction** is a short form of two words.

An **apostrophe** (') takes the place of the letters that are left out when two words are joined.

**Matt <u>did not</u> pick up his toys.**

↓

**Matt didn't pick up his toys.**

Remember to put the verb and *not* together to make a contraction.

| | | |
|---|---|---|
| **is not** ⟶ isn't | | **does not** → doesn't |
| **are not** → aren't | | **do not** ⟶ don't |
| **has not** → hasn't | | **did not** ⟶ didn't |
| **have not** → haven't | | **cannot** ⟶ can't |

**THINK AND WRITE**

**Verbs**

Why might you choose to use contractions in your writing? Write your answer in your journal.

## Guided Practice

**Tell how to make the words in ( ) into a contraction. Write the new word.**

1. Matt (cannot) find his book.

2. The book (is not) on his desk.

3. He (did not) put it on the shelf.

4. He (does not) know where it is.

5. He (has not) found the book yet.

---

**REVIEW** THE **RULES**

- A **contraction** is a short form of two words.
- An **apostrophe** takes the place of the letters that are left out.

---

## More Practice

**A.** **Write the contraction for the underlined words in each sentence.**

6. Matt <u>did not</u> clean his room.

7. The room <u>has not</u> been neat for days.

8. Matt's books <u>are not</u> on the shelf.

9. Matt's clothes <u>have not</u> been put away.

10. The clothes <u>do not</u> belong on the floor.

**B.** **Spiral Review** **Write the sentences. Correct the capitalization. Write the past tense of each verb in ( ).**

11. matt (look) under the bed.

12. he (lift) up a pile of clothes.

13. he (drop) a sweater on the floor.

14. then matt (pick) up the sweater.

15. at last he (spot) his book.

**Handbook**
**page 443, 453**

**Extra Practice**
**page 275**

---

**Writing Activity** **Paragraph**

Write a paragraph about a clean room and a messy room. How are they alike and different?
**APPLY GRAMMAR:** Use contractions in your paragraph.

# Apostrophes

---

**RULES**

An **apostrophe** (') takes the place of letters that are left out in a contraction.

**Marta didn't have skates.**

Add an apostrophe and **-s** to make a singular noun possessive. Add an apostrophe to make most plural nouns possessive.

**Marta's dad bought the girls' skates.**

---

Extra Practice page 276

## Practice

**A. Add the missing apostrophe in each underlined word.**

1. Gina <u>doesnt</u> save money.

2. <u>Ginas</u> bank is empty.

3. My bank <u>isnt</u> empty.

4. My <u>banks</u> slot is wide.

5. Both <u>brothers</u> banks are full.

**B.** **Spiral Review** **Write each sentence. Circle linking verbs. Underline each action verb.**

6. Susan saves seventy cents.

7. Nell's nine nickels are new.

8. Dan drops dimes on dishes.

9. Bobby's bank is big.

10. Connie counts coins quickly.

**THINK AND WRITE**

**Apostrophes**
Write to tell how you know if a word with an apostrophe is a contraction or a possessive noun.

# Verbs

— **REVIEW** THE **RULES** —

- Some verbs have special forms in the past tense.

  **go** →went   **say** —→said   **see** —→saw
  **run** →ran   **come** →came   **give** →gave

- A **contraction** is a short way to write two words. An apostrophe takes the place of the left-out letters.

## Practice

**Handbook**
**page 441**

**A. Write each sentence. Change each underlined verb to show past action.**

1. Yesterday Justin and I <u>go</u> to the shore.

2. We <u>come</u> to a tide pool.

3. I <u>see</u> a crab and <u>say</u>, "Wow!"

4. The crab <u>gives</u> Justin a fright.

5. Justin <u>runs</u> home.

**B.** Challenge **Write each sentence. Add an apostrophe to each underlined word.**

6. <u>Lin</u> class is visiting the pond.

7. The children see different <u>animals</u> homes.

8. The ducks <u>are not</u> in the water.

9. The teacher spots one <u>bird</u> nest.

10. The children <u>do not</u> want to get wet.

**Verbs**
Write five sentences.
Use a contraction
and the past-tense
form of *go*, *do*, *say*,
*see*, *run*, *come*, *give*,
or *sing*.

# Common Errors with Past-Tense Verbs

Some verbs have special spellings in the past tense. Sometimes a writer adds **-ed** to a verb instead of using the special spelling.

| Common Error | Examples | Corrected Sentences |
|---|---|---|
| Always adding -ed to form the past tense | He goed home. | He went home. |
| | A bird singed. | A bird sang. |

## THINK AND WRITE

**Verbs**

How is the past tense of the verb *run* different from the past tense of the verb *walk*? Write the answer in your journal.

**Troubleshooter**
**pages 426–427**

---

**REVIEW** THE **RULES**

**PAST-TENSE VERBS**

• Some verbs have special spellings to show the past tense.

• Remember Most past-tense verbs end with **-ed**.

---

## Practice

**Write each sentence. Use the past tense of the verb in ( ).**

**1.** My grandmother (comes) to my house.

**2.** I (run) to the door.

**3.** Grandmother (sees) me.

**4.** She (gives) me a present.

**5.** I (say) that I liked the gift.

228

## Practice

**A.** **Look at the encyclopedias on page 234. In what book would you find facts about these topics?**

1. dinosaur

2. Texas

3. elephant

4. Africa

5. whale

**B.** **Write the word you would look up for each name below.**

6. Thomas Jefferson

7. Betsy Ross

8. Helen Keller

9. Mark Twain

10. Maria Mitchell

### Writing Activity  A Report

Use an encyclopedia to look up information about your favorite animal. Write three sentences about the animal.

235

# Vocabulary: Suffixes

## DEFINITION

A **suffix** is a word part that is added to the end of a word. A suffix changes the meaning of the word.

| Suffix | Meaning | Examples |
|--------|---------|----------|
| -less | without | care + -less = careless |
| -ful | full of | care + -ful = careful |

Think about the meanings of the blue words in this paragraph.

*My little cousin Niles likes to be helpful. People think he is kind and thoughtful. But Niles is not very careful. In fact, he is quite careless. Even so, I am thankful for his help. He always tries hard.*

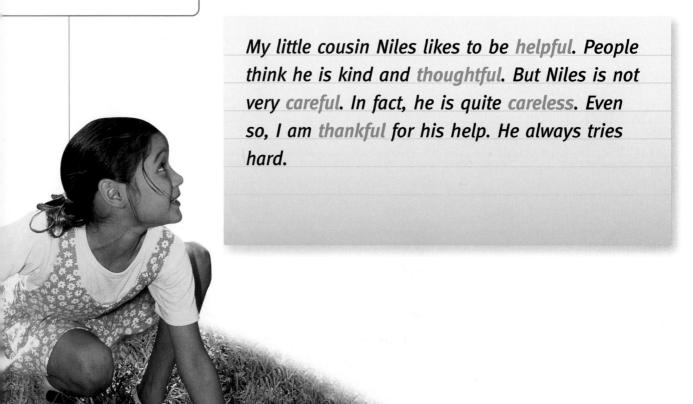

## Practice

**A.** **Write each word that has a suffix. Then write what the word means.**

**1.** At first, people are thankful.

**2.** They are never fearful of Niles.

**3.** They think little boys are harmless.

**4.** They are hopeful he will help.

**5.** They don't know he's not careful.

**B.** **Add *-less* and *-ful* to each of these words.**

**6.** color _____ _____

**7.** care _____ _____

**8.** hope _____ _____

**9.** use _____ _____

**10.** fear _____ _____

**C.** **Grammar Link** **11.–15. Write 5 sentences in the past tense. Use 5 of the new words from Practice B.**

**Writing Activity**    **A Character Description**

Describe a person you know who likes to help others. Use two words with the suffix *-ful* and two words with the suffix *-less*. Use long and short sentences.
**APPLY GRAMMAR:** Write in the present tense.

# Composition: Sentence Style and Variety

You can vary your sentences by making them different lengths or by using different beginning words.

---
### GUIDELINES

- Write sentences of different lengths.

- Do not begin every sentence in the same way.

- Combine the subjects or predicates of two sentences to make one sentence.
---

**THINK AND WRITE**

**Sentence Style and Variety**

How does using both short and long sentences make your writing more interesting? Write what you think.

See how this writer used varied sentences.

Manatees are called "sea cows." How are sea cows like farm cows? Farm cows live on land. Sea cows live in water. Cows on farms have four legs. Sea cows have one pair of flippers. Both animals are plant eaters. They graze. Farm cows graze in pastures. They eat grass and alfalfa. Sea cows graze in shallow water. They eat seaweed and sea grasses.

The sentences begin with different words.

The sentences vary in length.

Nouns were combined to form this sentence.

## Practice

**A.** **Write the sentences. Underline the part of each pair of sentences that is the same.**

**1.** Sea cows eat plants. Farm cows eat plants.

**2.** Farm cows live in meadows. Farm cows eat grass.

**3.** Sea cows live in the sea. Sea cows eat sea grass.

**4.** Farm cows are mammals. Sea cows are mammals.

**5.** Sea cows have flippers. Sea cows have a tail fin.

**B.** **Begin these sentences with different words or make them different lengths.**

**6.** My sister and I went to Florida.

**7.** My sister and I saw many things.

**8.** A whale leaped.

**9.** A whale dived.

**10.** My sister and I had fun.

**C.** **Grammar Link** **Use *and* to join the underlined words. Write the sentence.**

**11.** Sea cows are mammals. Whales are mammals.

**12.** Sea cows live in the sea. Whales live in the sea.

**13.** Both look like fish. Both never leave the water.

**14.** Both come to the surface. Both need to breathe air.

**15.** I love to see whales. I love to see sea cows.

**Writing Activity** **A Paragraph**

Write about a trip you took with friends or family.
**APPLY GRAMMAR:** Use linking verbs in your paragraph.

239

# Better Sentences

## Directions

Read the paragraph. Some parts are underlined. The underlined parts may be one of the following:

- **Incomplete sentences**
- **Correctly written sentences that should be combined**

Choose the best way to write each underlined part.

> ### Sample
>
> Look up in the sky! It's a horse. No, it's a dragon. <u>Maybe a throne for a king</u>. What you
> **(1)**
> see is a cloud picture. You can see anything you want in a cloud if you use your imagination.
>
> <u>A fluffy round shape could be a clown. A fluffy</u>
> **(2)**
> <u>round shape could be a sheep</u>. You can see a free show any time there are clouds in the sky.
> All you have to do is look up.

*A complete sentence has both a subject and a predicate.*

*Look out for sentences with words that can be combined to make one sentence.*

**1** ○ Maybe it is a throne for a king.

○ Maybe it is a throne. For a king.

○ Or maybe a throne for a king.

**2** ○ A fluffy round shape could be a clown could be a sheep.

○ A fluffy round clown or sheep.

○ A fluffy round shape could be a clown or a sheep.

**Test Tip**
Remember to read all the answer choices slowly and carefully.

240

# Vocabulary and Comprehension

## Directions

**Read the paragraph. Then read each question that follows the paragraph. Choose the best answer to each question.**

> **Sample**
>
> A zebra is not the same animal as a horse. They both have four legs and can run fast. Their bodies and heads look alike. But a zebra has stripes all over its body. Each has a mane, but the tails are different. A zebra has short hairs at the tip of its tail. A horse's tail is all long hairs. Also, people can ride a horse, but a zebra is not <u>playful</u> and won't like it if you try to go for a ride.

*Look for small word parts that help you understand the underlined word.*

**1** How are a zebra and a horse the same?

○ They have stripes.

○ They have long tails.

○ They have four legs and can run fast.

○ You can ride them both.

**2** The word <u>playful</u> in this paragraph means—

○ becoming angry

○ wanting to play

○ running quickly

○ wearing a saddle

# Seeing Like a Writer

There are many kinds of animals in the world. We can study them in real life or in pictures. When we do, we can see how they are alike and how they are different.

*My Friend* by Christian Pierre.

## ▶ How Things Are Different

Writing that compares gives different kinds of information about the same topic.

> Their mother is catching fish. Bears also eat fruit, nuts, berries, and, of course, honey.

These sentences tell what bears eat. What does the passage tell you bobcats eat?

## ▶ Comparing Words

Certain words tell readers that things are being compared. Use comparing words and phrases such as *but, also, like,* and *unlike.*

> When night comes, the bears are asleep inside a hollow tree on the ground. But it's time for the bobcat to go hunting.

## PRACTICE and APPLY

**Create a Category Chart**

1. Reread "Day School and Oak School."

2. List the kinds of information you learn.

3. List the facts about Day School.

4. List the facts about Oak School.

| Kind of Information | Day School | Oak School |
|---|---|---|
| | | |

# Prewrite

Writing that compares tells how two things are alike and different. You can compare people, places, or things.

## Purpose and Audience

The purpose of writing to compare might be to entertain or inform. Think about your audience. What do you want them to learn?

## Choose a Topic

Begin by **brainstorming**. Think of two things that are alike in some ways and different in other ways. **Explore and list** your ideas about the two things.

**THINK AND WRITE**

**Audience**
Write what you will have to do to make your audience feel interested in your topic.

*I explored my ideas about these two animals.*

Crocodiles and Alligators

long snouts

big tails

live near water

snouts look different

saw alligator in Florida

haven't seen a crocodile

are amazing

Notice how this writer used main ideas and details to tell how things are alike and different.

PREWRITE

DRAFT

REVISE

PROOFREAD

PUBLISH

### DRAFT

You see a big reptile with a long snout and tail. Is it an alligator or a crocodile? ·········· Main idea of first paragraph

Alligators and crocodiles ar different in some ways. ·········· Main idea of second paragraph

An alligator has a wide, stubby snout, and a crocodile's snout is narrow and pointed. A crocodiles bottom teeth show when ·········· Details tell more about each animal.

its mouth is closed.

Alligators and crocodiles are alike in some ·········· Main idea of third paragraph

ways. They live near water. Both of them are reptiles. They are both very interesting.

## PRACTICE and APPLY

### Draft Your Writing That Compares

1. Look at your prewriting chart again.

2. Write main ideas and details.

3. Tell how things are alike and different.

4. Use different kinds of sentences.

TIP!

## TECHNOLOGY

If you made your chart on the computer during prewriting, use the same document to start your draft. Turn each thing in your chart into a sentence. You can add more details later.

## Revise

**Writing** PROCESS

### Elaborate

One way to make your writing better is to elaborate. Add missing details to make the writing clearer.

> A crocodiles bottom teeth show when its
> *An alligator's teeth dont*
> mouth is closed. ∧

### COMPARE/ CONTRAST WORDS

one difference
same
but
also
alike
both

### Word Choice

What comparing words did this writer add to his article?

> Alligators and crocodiles are alike in some
> *both*
> ways. They live near the water.
> ∧

## Conferencing for the Reader

- Check to see if your partner's writing
  - explains how two things are alike
  - explains how two things are different
  - uses comparing and contrasting words
- Tell your partner what's good. And what you think needs to be changed.

254

## Better Sentences

Try to use different kinds of sentences. If a sentence sounds too long, you can make it into two sentences. See how this writer did that.

**PROOFREAD**

∧Teeth Tails and Snouts

You see a big reptile with a long snout and tail. Is it an alligator or a crocodile?

Alligators and crocodiles ar different in some ways. An alligator has a wide, stubby snout, and a crocodile's snout is narrow and pointed. A crocodiles bottom teeth show when its mouth is closed.∧ Another difference is the teeth. An alligator's teeth dont.

Alligators and crocodiles are alike in some ways. They live near water. Both of them are reptiles. They are both very interesting.

## PRACTICE and APPLY

### Revise Your Writing That Compares

1. Read your draft to yourself.

2. Share your draft with a partner.

3. Elaborate to make your writing better.

4. **Grammar** Did you write contractions correctly?

## Checklist ✓

**Revising**

- Did you think about your purpose and audience.

- Do the details tell about things that are alike and different?

- Did you use words that compare and contrast?

- Did you make your sentences different?

- Did you add a title?

255

# Proofread

Proofread your article after you revise it. Look for a different kind of mistake each time you read it.

**Writing** PROCESS

**Spelling**
Remember, the letter *q* is always followed by the letter *u*. (*quiet*)

**STRATEGIES FOR PROOFREADING**

- **Reread your writing several times.**
- **Reread for correct capitalization.**
- **Reread for correct punctuation.**
- **Make sure the contractions are correct.**
- **Check for correct spelling.** Look in the dictionary for words you are not sure about.

## REVIEW THE RULES

### GRAMMAR

- A contraction is a short form of two words. Write contractions by adding an apostrophe in place of letters that are left out.

### MECHANICS

- An apostrophe takes the place of the letters left out of a contraction.

- Apostrophes are also used to form possessives.

Look at the proofreading corrections. What does the ℃ mean? Why is this change needed?

PREWRITE

DRAFT

REVISE

**PROOFREAD**

PUBLISH

**REVISE**

∧Teeth，Tails，and Snouts

You see a big reptile with a long snout and tail. Is it an alligator or a crocodile?

*are*
Alligators and crocodiles ar different in
∧
some ways. An alligator has a wide, stubby

snout，and a crocodile's snout is narrow and
∧
*Another difference is the teeth.*
pointed. A crocodiles bottom teeth show when
∧
*An alligator's teeth dont.*
its mouth is closed.∧

Alligators and crocodiles are alike in some
*both*
ways. They live near water. Both of them are
∧
reptiles. They are both very interesting.

**Checklist ✓**
**Proofreading**
- ■ Did you spell all words correctly?
- ■ Did you use capital letters correctly?
- ■ Did you write contractions correctly?
- ■ Did you indent all paragraphs?

**PROOFREADING MARKS**

| | |
|---|---|
| ♯ | new paragraph |
| ∧ | add |
| ℃ | take out |
| ≡ | Make a capital letter. |
| / | Make a small letter. |
| ⑤℗ | Check the spelling. |
| ⊙ | Add a period. |

## PRACTICE and APPLY

**Proofread Your Writing That Compares**

1. Fix spelling mistakes.

2. Check capital letters and punctuation.

3. Check how apostrophes are used.

4. Indent paragraphs.

# Publish

Review your writing again before you publish it. This checklist can help.

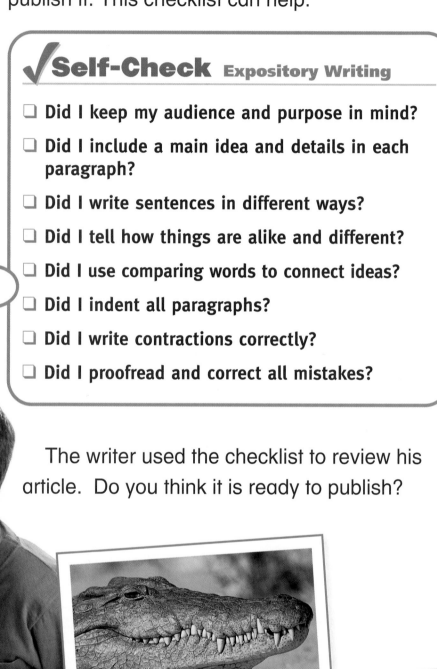

✓ **Self-Check** Expository Writing

❏ Did I keep my audience and purpose in mind?

❏ Did I include a main idea and details in each paragraph?

❏ Did I write sentences in different ways?

❏ Did I tell how things are alike and different?

❏ Did I use comparing words to connect ideas?

❏ Did I indent all paragraphs?

❏ Did I write contractions correctly?

❏ Did I proofread and correct all mistakes?

The writer used the checklist to review his article. Do you think it is ready to publish?

# Teeth, Tails, and Snouts

## by Matt Cooper

You see a huge reptile with a long snout and tail. Is it an alligator or a crocodile?

Alligators and crocodiles are different in some ways. An alligator has a wide, stubby snout. A crocodile's snout is narrow and pointed. Another difference is the teeth. A crocodile's bottom teeth show when its mouth is closed. An alligator's teeth don't.

Alligators and crocodiles are alike in some ways. They both live near water. Both of them are reptiles. They are both very interesting.

### TIP!

**Handwriting**

Put all the letters in a single word close together and leave space before and after the word. This way the reader can tell when a word begins and ends.

## PRACTICE and APPLY

### Publish Your Writing That Compares

1. Check your revised draft one more time.

2. Make a neat final copy.

3. Add drawings or pictures.

# Present Your Writing That Compares

**Before you present your article, you need to plan.**

## STEP 1

### How to Explain Your Article

**Strategies for Speaking** Your purpose is to entertain and inform. As you speak, help your audience "see" the things you are comparing.

- Write main ideas on cards. Add notes to help you remember details.
- Speak in a clear, loud voice.
- Remember to smile and relax.
- Plan to leave some time for your listeners to ask questions.

**TiP!**

### Listening Strategies

- **Set a purpose. Listen to find out information, for enjoyment, or both.**

- **Try to picture how things are alike and different.**

- **Don't interrupt.**

- **Keep your eyes on the speaker.**

## Multimedia Ideas

Does your classroom have an overhead projector? If so, you might show drawings that tell about facts in your article.

## STEP 2

# How to Show Your Article

**Suggestions for Visuals**

Show pictures or objects.

- Drawings and photos can show how things are alike and different.
- A diagram can show facts.
- Models made from clay can show how things really look.

## STEP 3

# How to Share Your Article

**Strategies for Rehearsing** Be sure to practice before you give your presentation.

- Practice speaking in front of a mirror.
- Make an audiotape of your speech. Do you need to speak more slowly?
- Ask a friend to listen and give you tips.

**Viewing Strategies**

- Study the materials on display.

- Ask yourself how the pictures and diagrams can help you understand information.

- Look for details that are not in the speech.

## PRACTICE and APPLY

**Present Your Writing That Compares**

1. Make notes about what you want to say.

2. Use pictures, photographs, or diagrams to show important points.

3. Practice alone or with a friend.

4. Relax and give your ideas clearly.

# Writing Tests

Remember to read the prompt on a writing test carefully. Look for key words and phrases that tell you what to write about and how to do your writing.

> *Sometimes a prompt does not name the audience.*

> *Look for words that tell the purpose of the writing.*

> *Look for words that tell what kind of writing this is.*

**Prompt**

Think about what you know about a house cat and a lion.

Write one or two paragraphs describing a house cat and a lion. Give <u>details and facts</u> telling <u>how they are alike and how they are different.</u>

## How to Read a Prompt

**Purpose**  Look for key words that tell you the purpose of the writing. The words "details and facts" tell you that the purpose of this writing is to inform. When you use details and facts, you are informing your audience.

**Audience**  When the prompt does not tell who the audience is, you can think of your teacher as the audience.

**Writing to Compare**  The words "how they are alike and how they are different" tell you that this will be the kind of writing that compares two things. When you write to compare two things, you use facts and details to tell how they are alike and different.

**Test Tip**
Remember to read the prompt carefully before you begin to write.

**Write a short biography** Have you ever wondered who invented such things as earmuffs, the basketball, zippers, or ballpoint pens? Choose an invention. Then find out about the inventor.

Write about the inventor. Include some interesting facts about the person's life.

**PROJECT 2**

## A Scrapbook

It's hard to believe that a 300-pound panda only weighed four ounces at birth. How much have you changed since you were born?

**Growing and Changing**
Create a scrapbook about yourself called "Then and Now." Write about how you are the same and different now. Include photos.

## Extra Practice

# The Verb *Be*

**A. Write each sentence. Write the word that is a form of *be*.**

1. I am glad to hear from you.
2. How are you?
3. How is camp?
4. Friday was cold.
5. Saturday and Sunday were rainy.
6. We were inside all weekend.
7. I was ready to go home.
8. Today is much better.
9. The sun is out.
10. We are ready to go on a hike.

**B. Write each sentence. Draw a line under the correct form of *be*.**

11. Tonight the moon (is, were) full.
12. Tonight the stars (are, is) bright.
13. Yesterday it (were, was) foggy.
14. Last night the stars (was, were) dim.
15. Now the sky (is, are) clear.

# Helping Verbs

**A. Write the underlined word that is a helping verb in each sentence.**

1. I <u>am</u> <u>planning</u> a surprise.

2. My brother <u>is</u> <u>helping</u>.

3. We <u>are</u> <u>fixing</u> breakfast.

4. Mom and Dad <u>are</u> <u>sleeping</u>.

5. Dan and Ben <u>have</u> <u>set</u> the table.

6. Juan <u>is</u> <u>making</u> the juice.

7. He <u>has</u> <u>squeezed</u> the oranges.

8. I <u>am</u> <u>stirring</u> the oatmeal.

9. Juan <u>has</u> <u>buttered</u> the toast.

10. Mom and Dad <u>have</u> <u>come</u> downstairs.

**B. Write each sentence. Draw a line under the helping verb.**

11. Mom and Dad are smiling at us.

12. They have just finished breakfast.

13. Dan has cleared the table.

14. Jim is loading the dishwasher.

15. I am planning the next surprise.

## Extra Practice

# Linking Verbs

**A. Write *L* if the underlined verb is a *linking* verb. Write *A* if it is an *action* verb.**

1. I <u>am</u> a bird-watcher.

2. My favorite bird <u>is</u> the bluebird.

3. Sometimes a robin <u>sits</u> on our windowsill.

4. Robins <u>are</u> brown.

5. A robin <u>lives</u> in our yard.

6. The bird <u>makes</u> a chirping sound.

7. Some birds <u>eat</u> tiny insects.

8. Bluebirds <u>are</u> pretty.

9. Today I <u>saw</u> a bluebird.

10. I <u>took</u> a picture of the bluebird.

**B. Write the sentence. Circle the verb. Then write *linking verb* or *action verb*.**

11. I am a nature lover.

12. I bought a hummingbird feeder.

13. The bird feeder was in my garden.

14. Robins come every day.

15. Birds are fun to watch.

# Commas in Names of Places

**A. Write each place name. Put a comma between the name of each city and each state.**

1. Tiffin Ohio

2. San Jose California

3. Dewey Beach Delaware

4. Cape May New Jersey

5. Houston Texas

6. Orlando Florida

7. Las Vegas Nevada

8. Norman Oklahoma

9. Jackson Mississippi

10. Chicago Illinois

**B. Write each sentence. Put a comma in the correct place.**

11. Let's visit Denver Colorado.

12. We'll fly from Ann Arbor Michigan.

13. We can drive to Provo Utah.

14. I'd like to see Seattle Washington.

15. I'm thinking about going to Atlanta Georgia.

271

# Grammar

## The Verbs *Go* and *Do*

**A.** Choose the word in ( ) that tells about action in the past. Write each sentence.

1. Mom and I (go, went) to the city.

2. We (went, go) by bus.

3. Mom (did, does) some shopping.

4. What (do, did) you buy?

5. I (do, did) not buy a thing.

6. Then we (went, go) to lunch.

7. I (do, did) not know what to eat.

8. After lunch we (go, went) to a movie.

9. My sister (does, did) not come along.

10. My sister (did, does) her homework instead.

**B.** Change the verb in ( ) to show action in the past. Write each sentence.

11. Mom and I (go) home after the movie.

12. We (do) not take the bus.

13. We (go) by train instead.

14. We (do) not get home until late.

15. I (go) right to bed.

# The Verbs *Say*, *See*, and *Run*

**A.** **Change the underlined verb to tell about an action in the past. Write the sentence.**

1. Mom <u>says</u>, "Please walk Rags."

2. My sister and I <u>say</u>, "Okay."

3. Our dog <u>sees</u> a squirrel.

4. Rags <u>runs</u> after the squirrel.

5. My sister <u>says</u>, "Let's follow him."

6. Rags <u>runs</u> through the yards.

7. We <u>run</u> after him.

8. Our friend Ben <u>sees</u> us.

9. He <u>says</u>, "I'll help you."

10. We <u>see</u> Rags down the street.

**B.** **Change the verbs to tell about an action in the past. Write the sentence.**

11. I see the squirrel.

12. The animal runs up a tree.

13. We run toward the tree.

14. We finally see Rags!

15. We all say, "Hooray!"

## Extra Practice

# The Verbs *Come*, *Give*, and *Sing*

**A. Change the underlined verb to tell about an action in the past. Write the sentence.**

1. The Fourth of July <u>comes</u> at last.

2. We <u>give</u> a big party in the backyard.

3. Everyone in the family <u>comes</u> to the party.

4. Grandma from Texas <u>comes</u>, too.

5. The family <u>sings</u> songs about America.

6. Later, Grandpa <u>gives</u> a speech.

7. We <u>give</u> Grandpa a big cheer.

8. Our friends <u>come</u> over with a pie.

9. Then we <u>sing</u> a special song we wrote.

10. Grandpa <u>sings</u> loudest of all!

**B. Change the verbs to tell about an action in the past. Write the sentence.**

11. My aunt and uncle come late.

12. Uncle Mike gives me a hug.

13. Aunt Nancy comes from far away.

14. Everyone sings one last song.

15. Then we give thanks for America.

# Contractions with *not*

**A.** **Write each sentence. Circle each contraction.**

1. Tina can't find Sage.

2. The cat didn't touch her food.

3. Sage doesn't come when Tina calls.

4. It isn't like Sage to get lost.

5. Mom and Dad aren't worried.

6. "Don't worry," say Mom and Dad.

7. Sage hasn't run away.

8. Sage isn't hurt.

9. Tina hasn't seen the kittens.

10. "Don't forget to look in the tree," says Mom.

**B.** **Write each sentence. Write a contraction for the words in ( ).**

11. Tina (cannot) believe how small the kittens are.

12. "(Are not) they cute?" asks Mom.

13. "Why (did not) the kittens want to eat?" asked Tina.

14. Sage (has not) eaten all her food.

15. "Why (do not) you get her milk?" says Mom.

275

## Extra Practice

# Apostrophes

**A.** **Write the underlined word. Add an apostrophe.**

1. <u>Sues</u> sandwich is tasty.

2. Cora <u>cant</u> cook carrots.

3. <u>Idas</u> uncle eats rice.

4. Lizzy <u>isnt</u> hungry.

5. <u>Daves</u> dad drove to the store.

6. They <u>didnt</u> have any more corn.

7. Mr. <u>Stones</u> cart was empty.

8. Harry <u>hasnt</u> heard from Hanna.

9. Fran fed <u>Freds</u> fish.

10. Arthur and Arnold <u>arent</u> at home.

**B. Write the sentence. Add an apostrophe.**

11. Willy wears Wallys watch.

12. Petes paintings are pretty.

13. Sids sister sips soup.

14. Donnas dog likes to dig.

15. Tims truck is a tanker.

16. Hans hasnt had a hamburger.

17. Petes pet parrot is in a parade.

18. Jim and Jenna dont like to juggle.

19. Carmen cant copy Carrie.

20. Allie and Alice arent always on time.

# Pronouns and Expository Writing

In this unit you will learn about pronouns. You will also learn how to give facts and information in your writing.

**Science Link**  Sam is putting something important together, piece by piece.  What is it?

Sam spends hours and hours digging for fossils. Once, Sam found a few tiny pieces of bone. Sam knew he had found something important. So he spent the day on his hands and knees looking for more bone. He picked up all the tiny pieces he could find. Then he glued them together. The pieces made up a dinosaur tooth. The dinosaur had lived millions of years ago!

"Are You a Fossil Fan?" from *Time for Kids*

## Thinking Like a Writer

**Expository Writing**
Expository writing gives facts and information about a topic.

• What facts add up to the main idea of the passage?

**Pronouns** These words take the place of nouns.

 **QUICK WRITE**
Write the pronouns in the passage above.

# Pronouns

**Pronouns** take the place of nouns. Pronouns tell about one person or thing.

Tina **grows corn. She sells corn.**

Pronouns also can tell about more than one person or thing.

The apples **are ripe. They taste good.**

Pronouns must match the words they replace. Look at the chart to see which pronouns replace which words.

| One Person or Thing | | | More Than One | |
|---|---|---|---|---|
| she | he | it | they | we |
| ↓ | ↓ | ↓ | ↓ | ↓ |
| Eva | Ed | apple | Eva and Ed | Ed and I |

## THiNK AND WRITE

**Pronouns**

Why might you use pronouns instead of nouns in your writing? Write the answer.

## Guided Practice

**Write a pronoun to take the place of the underlined words.**

**1.** Mom and I are farmers.

**2.** Mom sells apples to the market.

**3.** Mr. Ray owns the market.

**4.** Mom and Ray talk about apples.

**5.** Apples will be on sale today.

---

**REVIEW** THE **RULES**

- A **pronoun** takes the place of one or more nouns.

- Pronouns must match the noun or nouns they replace.

---

## More Practice

**A. Write each sentence. Write pronouns to replace the underlined words.**

6. <u>Troy's Fruit Store</u> sells fresh fruits.

7. <u>Grandma and Grandpa</u> shop there.

8. <u>Grandpa and I</u> pick out peaches.

9. <u>A peach</u> is a fruit.

10. <u>Grandma</u> buys some apples.

**Handbook**
page 442

**Extra Practice**
page 336

**B.** `Spiral Review` **Write the letter. Choose the correct verb in ( ) to show past action. Circle each pronoun.**

**11.–15.** Dear Grandma,

How are you? Yesterday Dad and I (go, went) to the fair. We (see, saw) so many things!

Love,
Arthur

---

**Writing Activity  A Paragraph**

Write a paragraph about a family activity.

**APPLY GRAMMAR:** Use pronouns in your paragraph.

# I and Me

Use the pronouns **I** and **me** to tell about yourself.

Use **I** in the subject of a sentence.

**Paul and I learn about the sun.**

Use **me** after an action verb.

**The teacher asks me a question.**

Look at the chart to see where *I* and *me* are used in sentences.

| In the Subject | After the Verb |
|---|---|
| Dad and I read a book. | Dad shows me pictures. |
| ↑ subject | ↑ action verb |

**THINK AND WRITE**

**Pronouns**

How do you know when to use *I* and when to use *me*? Write your answer.

## Guided Practice

**Choose *I* or *me* to complete each sentence.**

**1.** My dad teaches (I, me) about the sun.

**2.** Dad and (I, me) read about of the sun.

**3.** The sun makes (I, me) feel warm.

**4.** Dad tells (I, me) interesting facts.

**5.** Now (I, me) know more about the sun.

## REVIEW THE RULES

- Use **I** to tell about yourself in the subject of a sentence. Use **me** after an action verb.

## More Practice

**A.** Choose the correct pronoun in ( ). Then write each sentence.

**6.** (I, me) will write a science report.

**7.** Mrs. Sing gives (I, me) a book.

**8.** Amy and (I, me) read the book.

**9.** Amy helps (I, me) with my notes.

**10.** Now (I, me) can write my report.

**Handbook**
**page 442**

**B.** Spiral Review Write each sentence. Replace the words in ( ) with the correct pronoun. Circle each helping verb.

**Extra**
**Practice**
**page 337**

**11.** (The children) have started a garden.

**12.** (Sarah) has planted some seeds.

**13.** (Mike) has not planted any seeds yet.

**14.** (Suki and I) are growing beans.

**15.** (The sun) is shining on our plants.

## Writing Activity  An Invitation

Write to invite a friend to do something with you.
**APPLY GRAMMAR:** Use *I* and *me* in your invitation.

# We and Us

## RULES

Use **we** and **us** to talk about yourself and another person.

Jill and I **play ball.**     **Mom watches**

↓                          Jill and me.

                                     ↓

**We play ball.**       **Mom watches us.**

Use we in the subject of a sentence. Use us after an action verb.

| In the Subject | After the Verb |
|---|---|
| <u>We</u> like soccer. | Dad <u>took</u> us to a game. |
| ↑ | ↑ |
| *subject* | *action verb* |

**Pronouns**

How do you know when to use *we* and when to use *us*? Write your answer.

## Guided Practice

**Choose *we* or *us* to replace the underlined words.**

1. <u>Jill and I</u> run fast and kick the ball.

2. Rico sees <u>Jill and me</u>.

3. <u>Rico, Jill, and I</u> play ball together.

4. Jill gives <u>Rico and me</u> the ball.

5. <u>Rico and I</u> kick the ball to each other.

284

## REVIEW THE RULES

- Use **we** in the subject to talk about yourself and others. Use **us** after an action verb.

## More Practice

**A. Write each sentence. Write _we_ or _us_ in place of the underlined words.**

6. Fran teaches <u>Rita and me</u> to swim.

7. <u>Rita and I</u> have fun.

8. <u>Fran, Rita, and I</u> swim at the pool.

9. Fran's sister likes <u>Rita and me</u>.

10. Fay takes <u>Fran, Rita, and me</u> to the beach.

**B.** **Spiral Review** **Write the paragraph. Choose the correct pronoun in ( ). Add apostrophes.**

11.–15. Come and see (I, me) play ball. Today (I, me) play at my schools playground. My friends and (I, me) play ball almost every day. We cant wait for our big game!

**Handbook**
**page 442**

**Extra Practice**
**page 338**

**Writing Activity** **A Description**

Write about what you do to stay healthy. Include important details.

**APPLY GRAMMAR:** Use the pronouns _we_ and _us_.

 **Health Link**

**Grammar**

# Using *I* and *Me*

> **RULES**
>
> The pronoun **I** is always a capital letter.
>
> **Luis and I will make a bird house.**
>
> Name yourself last when talking about yourself and another person.
>
> **Dad will help Luis and me.**

**Extra Practice**
page 339

**THINK AND WRITE**

**Pronouns**

Why is it important to use a capital letter when you write *I*?

## Practice

**A.** **Tell if the sentence uses *I* or *me* correctly. If it does not, correct the sentence.**

1. Luis and i go outside.

2. Dad follows me and Luis.

3. I and Luis work with Dad.

4. Dad shows Luis and me what to do.

5. Dad, Luis, and i made a bird house.

**B.** **Spiral Review** **Write each sentence. Replace underlined words with pronouns. Then write *statement*, *question*, *command*, or *exclamation*.**

6. Come with <u>Grandpa and me</u>.

7. <u>Grandpa and I</u> will show you the ducks.

8. <u>Two ducks</u> live near the pond.

9. Can <u>Grandpa</u> see the ducks' nest?

10. How high <u>the duck</u> flies!

# Pronouns

## REVIEW THE RULES

- A **pronoun** takes the place of one or more nouns. Pronouns match the nouns they replace.

- Use *I* in the subject of a sentence. Use *me* after an action verb. Use *we* in the subject of a sentence. Use *us* after an action verb.

- Name yourself last when talking about yourself and another person.

## Practice

**Handbook**
**page 442**

**A. Write each sentence. Write pronouns to replace the underlined words.**

1. <u>Grandma</u> lives near a rain forest.

2. Grandma takes <u>Luke and me</u> there.

3. <u>Luke and I</u> hear the birds.

4. <u>Luke</u> sees a big parrot.

5. <u>The parrot</u> has green feathers.

**B. Challenge Write the sentences. Change the words in ( ) to make each sentence correct.**

6. (Me and Kate) pretend to be in the rain forest.

7. A big tiger surprises (Kate and I).

8. (The tiger, I, and Kate) stand very still.

9. (Kate and i) like the tiger.

10. He doesn't bother (me and Kate).

**QUICK WRITE**

**Pronouns**
Write 5 sentences. Use different pronouns in each sentence. Use *I*, *me*, *we*, and *us* correctly.

# Pronoun-Verb Agreement

Pronouns and verbs must agree, or work together, in sentences.

When the pronoun **he, she,** or **it** is in the subject of a sentence, add **-s** to most verbs in the present tense. When the pronoun is **I, you, we,** or **they,** do not add **-s.**

| Pam play**s** tag. | Mark and I play, too. |
| ↓ | ↓ |
| She play**s** tag. | We play, too. |

See how the verb goes with the pronoun in the subject of the sentence.

| One Person or Thing | More Than One |
|---|---|
| I/You hide | We/You hide |
| He/She/It hides | They hide |

## THINK AND WRITE

**Pronouns**

How do you know when to add -s to a verb? Write your answer in your journal.

## Guided Practice

**Name the correct verb in ( ).**

**1.** He (run, runs) to Masako.

**2.** They (sit, sits) by the door.

**3.** We (see, sees) Jess behind the tree.

**4.** You (stay, stays) near the fence.

**5.** I (race, races) to the goal.

---

**REVIEW THE RULES**

• If a pronoun in the subject is singular, add -*s* to the verb. If it is *I, you,* or plural, do not add -*s*.

---

**More Practice**

**A.** **Choose the correct verb in ( ) in each sentence. Then write the sentence.**

6. I (learn, learns) how to roller-skate.

7. You (hold, holds) my hand.

8. He (give, gives) me some good advice.

9. She (run, runs) beside me.

10. Then we (skate, skates) together.

**B.** [Spiral Review] **Choose the correct form of the verb in ( ). Then write each sentence and circle the subject.**

11. Holly and Bill (come, comes) to our party.

12. My brother (do, does) a funny trick.

13. Aunt Pat (give, gives) Joe a present.

14. I (say, says) "hello" to everyone.

15. We (sing, sings) and clap our hands.

**Handbook**
**page 442**

**Extra Practice page 340**

---

**Writing Activity**   **A Clapping Chant**

Write a song you can sing in a clapping game.
**APPLY GRAMMAR:** Circle each pronoun in your song.

 **Music Link**

# Possessive Pronouns

**RULES**

A **possessive pronoun** takes the place of a possessive noun. A possessive pronoun shows who owns or has something.

<u>Sarah's</u> **family is going to Washington, D.C.**
↓
**Her family is going to Washington, D.C.**

A possessive pronoun can take the place of a possessive noun.

| One Person or Thing | More Than One |
|---|---|
| my | our |
| your | your |
| his, her, its | their |

**THINK AND WRITE**

**Pronouns**

How can you tell when to use the word *his* or the word *her*? Write your answer.

## Guided Practice

**Write a possessive pronoun to replace the underlined words.**

**1.** <u>People's</u> voices seem loud in the hall.

**2.** Mom holds <u>my sister's</u> hand.

**3.** We listen to <u>a man's</u> voice on tape.

**4.** <u>The Capitol's</u> rooms have many paintings.

**5.** <u>Mom's</u> postcard is beautiful.

---

**REVIEW THE RULES**

- Use a **possessive pronoun** to show who owns something.

---

### More Practice

**A.** Write each sentence. Write a possessive pronoun for the underlined words.

**6.** The <u>museum's</u> rooms are big.

**7.** Today <u>the visitors'</u> guide is Ms. Hunt.

**8.** My family likes <u>Ms. Hunt's</u> tour.

**9.** The <u>room's</u> furniture is so interesting!

**10.** My <u>brother's</u> feet are getting tired.

**Handbook**
**page 443**

**Extra Practice**
**page 341**

**B.** **Spiral Review** Write each sentence. Replace the underlined words with *we* or *us.* Add a comma in the name of a place.

**11.** Dad takes <u>Mom, Josh, and me</u> to Arlington Virginia.

**12.** <u>My friend and I</u> like the space museum.

**13.** My mom shows <u>Josh and me</u> a rocket.

**14.** <u>Mom, Josh, and I</u> see a special movie.

**15.** The movie thrills <u>Josh and me</u>!

**Writing Activity** **A Biography**

Write a paragraph about a famous person from the past. Put your sentences in a clear order.

**APPLY GRAMMAR:** Use possessive pronouns.

**Social Studies Link**

291

# Contractions: Pronoun and Verb

A **contraction** is the short form of two words.

An **apostrophe** (') takes the place of the letters that are left out when the words are combined.

<u>I am</u> **thinking of a riddle.**

↓

**I'm thinking of a riddle.**

See which letter each apostrophe replaces.

| Singular | | Plural | |
|---|---|---|---|
| I am | = I'm | We are | = We're |
| You are | = You're | You are | = You're |
| She is | = She's | They are | = They're |
| He is | = He's | | |
| It is | = It's | | |

**THINK AND WRITE**

**Contractions**

Why do you use an apostrophe when you write a contraction? Write the answer.

## Guided Practice

**Write each sentence. Change the underlined words to a contraction.**

1. <u>We are</u> making up math riddles.

2. <u>She is</u> helping, too.

3. <u>He is</u> telling a riddle to the class.

4. <u>They are</u> figuring out the riddle.

5. <u>I am</u> ready for another riddle.

---
REVIEW THE RULES
---

- A **contraction** is a short form of two words.

- An **apostrophe** (') takes the place of the letters that are left out in the contraction.

## More Practice

**A.** **Write each sentence. Write the contraction that replaces the underlined words.**

6. <u>I am</u> thinking of a number.

7. <u>You are</u> asking me five questions.

8. <u>It is</u> a number under twenty.

9. <u>They are</u> guessing the number.

10. <u>She is</u> right!

**B.** **Spiral Review** **Write the sentences. Correct the words in ( ). Circle each action verb.**

11. (Me and Ellie) write riddles.

12. Our dad helps (Ellie and I).

13. (Dad, I, and Ellie) like riddles.

14. Ellie asks (me and Dad) a new riddle.

15. (Dad and i) guess the answer.

**Handbook**
page 443

**Extra Practice**
page 342

---
**Writing Activity** **Riddle**

Write a riddle about an animal.
**APPLY GRAMMAR:** Use contractions in your riddle.

293

**Grammar**

# Contractions and Possessive Pronouns

---

**RULES**

An **apostrophe** takes the place of letters left out in a contraction.

> **You're** a pilot.

A possessive pronoun never has an apostrophe.

> **Your** job is to fly the plane.

---

**Extra Practice page 343**

**THINK AND WRITE**

**Pronouns**

Why are *it's/its, you're/your,* and *they're/their* harder to tell apart in speaking than in writing?

## Practice

**A.** **Name the correct word in ( ).**

**1.** Look at the plane. (It's, Its) wings are huge!

**2.** (They're, Their) checking the plane.

**3.** (They're, Their) job is important.

**4.** (You're, Your) seat is next to mine.

**5.** Now (you're, your) ready to fly.

**B.** **Spiral Review** **Write the sentences. Make each verb in ( ) agree with each subject. Replace the underlined words with possessive pronouns.**

**6.–10.** Mrs. Fox (work) at my school. She (take) care of <u>the school's</u> computers. <u>Mrs. Fox's</u> tools (is) in a special kit.

# Pronouns

— **REVIEW** THE **RULES** —

- A **present-tense** verb must go with the pronoun in the subject of the sentence.

- Use **possessive pronouns** to take the place of possessive nouns.

- A **contraction** is a short form of two words. A **possessive pronoun** never has an apostrophe.

**Handbook**
**page 442–443**

## Practice

**A.** Write each sentence. Write the correct form of the word in ( ).

1. We (like, likes) jigsaw puzzles.

2. Sometimes (we, our) puzzles are hard.

3. She always (find, finds) the pieces.

4. She shows me (she, her) plan.

5. I (fit, fits) the pieces together, too.

**B.** ⬛ **Challenge** ⬛ Write the sentences. Choose the correct word in ( ).

6. (You're, Your) mom fixes cars.

7. She says (it's, its) not a hard job.

8. Mom fixes (they're, their) tire.

9. (It's, Its) hole needs a patch.

10. (They're, Their) happy with the work.

**Pronouns**
Write 5 sentences. Use pronouns, possessive pronouns, and pronoun-verb contractions.

# Common Errors with Pronouns

Sometimes writers use the wrong pronoun as the subject of a sentence or after an action verb.

| Common Error | Example | Corrected Sentence |
| --- | --- | --- |
| Using me or us as the subject of a sentence | Bob and me play. | Bob and I play. |
| Using I or we in the predicate | Dad watches Bob and I. | Dad watches Bob and me. |

**Troubleshooter**
**pages 428–429**

**THINK AND WRITE**

**Pronouns**

How do you know when to use *I* or *me* in a sentence? Write the answer in your journal.

**REVIEW** THE **RULES**

**PRONOUNS**

- Use *I* or *we* as the subject of a sentence.
- Use *me* or *us* after an action verb.

## Practice

Write each sentence. Choose the correct pronoun in ( ).

**1.** Ms. Han paints with Ken and (I, me).

**2.** Ken and (I, me) make a big picture.

**3.** (We, Us) hang it in the main hallway.

**4.** My grandma visits Ms. Han and (we, us).

**5.** Ken and (I, me) show him the picture.

# Mechanics and Spelling

## Directions

Read the paragraph and decide which type of mistake, if any, appears in each underlined part. Choose the correct answer. If there is no mistake, choose "No mistake."

**Sample**

I lost a book that I had borrowed from

the library. Dad and i searched the house for it.
   (1)

Dad finally found it. My little brothers had
(2)

put it in they're room.
(3)

*Check to see if any of the underlined words need to be capitalized.*

*A possessive pronoun is never spelled with an apostrophe.*

*Does the underlined part have any mistakes? Sometimes there is no mistake.*

**1** ○ Spelling
○ Capitalization
○ Punctuation
○ No mistake

**2** ○ Spelling
○ Capitalization
○ Punctuation
○ No mistake

**3** ○ Spelling
○ Capitalization
○ Punctuation
○ No mistake

**Test Tip**
Remember, read all of the answers before you make your choice.

# TIME FOR KIDS Writer's Notebook

**RESEARCH**

**RESEARCH** If I am looking for information in a book, I turn to the book's **index**. The index lists everything that is in the book. It also gives the page numbers where I can find the information. The index is in ABC order. It is at the end of a book.

**COMPOSITION SKILLS**

**WRITING WELL** The **main idea** of a story is what the story is about. But when I write, I need to say more than the main idea. I want to "paint a picture" with words. These "word pictures" are called **details**. Details bring my story to life!

**VOCABULARY SKILLS**

**USING WORDS** Smart, bright, clever are words that mean the same. These words are **synonyms**. Synonyms help make my stories more interesting. They also help me say just what I want to say. Can you think of any synonyms for the word pretty?

## Read Now!

As you read the photo essay, write down the main idea. Then write down some details that make the story more interesting to you.

# TIME
## FOR KIDS
### PHOTO ESSAY

# Cry of the Wolf

**Gray wolves have returned to Yellowstone National Park. Will they be able to stay there?**

# Cry of the Wolf

For a long time, gray wolves lived in the forests of the U.S. West. Then, in the 1800s, farmers and ranchers moved in. Wolves sometimes killed farmers' animals. People worried that wolves might kill humans too. So wolves were shot. By the early 1930s, no wolves were left in Yellowstone Park's woods.

In 1995, 31 wolves were caught in Canada. They were sent to Yellowstone. The animals did well.

But many ranchers and farmers think the wolves might kill their animals. People are coming up with a plan to keep the farmers happy and the wolves in Yellowstone.

Cover: Darren Bennett/Animals Animals
All photos William Campbell

Scientists put a radio collar on a wild wolf pup. The radio signals help park workers keep track of the wolves. If a wolf makes trouble for a rancher, it can be moved.

interNET CONNECTION Go to www.mhschool.com/language-arts for more information on the topic.

## Practice

**A.** Write *yes* if the underlined words are synonyms. Write *no* if they are not.

**1.** I <u>like</u> mysteries and <u>enjoy</u> solving them.

**2.** This <u>hard</u> riddle is <u>difficult</u> to figure out.

**3.** I wondered how the <u>healthy</u> pet got <u>sick</u>.

**4.** The <u>old</u> trick was <u>new</u> to me.

**5.** The movie <u>ended</u> with a surprise <u>finish</u>.

**B.** Copy each sentence. Use a synonym from the box in place of the underlined word.

> small      tall      glad      caring      large

**6.** My mom is a <u>kind</u> person.

**7.** Mom was <u>happy</u> to help my uncle.

**8.** My uncle has a <u>tiny</u> dog.

**9.** The dog chases <u>huge</u> cars.

**10.** They built a <u>high</u> fence.

**C.** **Grammar Link** **11.–15.** Rewrite the sentences from practice B. Replace nouns with pronouns. Use different synonyms.

### Writing Activity   Sentence Pairs

Write pairs of sentences about something you had to figure out. Use synonyms in your sentences.

**APPLY GRAMMAR:** Use one pronoun in each pair.

305

# Composition: Main Idea and Supporting Details

Good writers use a main idea sentence to tell the most important idea in a paragraph. They write details to support the main idea.

**THINK AND WRITE**

**Main Idea and Supporting Details**
Write about why details must support the main idea.

---

**GUIDELINES**

- A **main idea** is the most important idea in a piece of writing.

- **Supporting details** tell more about the main idea.

- All the sentences in a **paragraph** should tell about one main idea.

---

Notice the main idea and details in this paragraph.

*A main idea sentence states the most important idea.*

*Detail sentences give more information about the main idea.*

> Colonial Americans had many problems that we don't have today. There was no electricity. Candles gave dim light. Cooking was not easy because it had to be done in a fireplace. Many things had to be made by hand. It was hard work. Often people would raise sheep for wool. Then they would spin the wool into yarn and weave it into material for clothes.

## Practice

**A.** Write *yes* or *no* to tell if each sentence supports the main idea.

> **Main Idea:** Settlers in America built different kinds of houses.

1. Early homes looked like cottages.

2. Most furniture was made of wood.

3. Stone homes were built in New England.

4. Pioneers built log cabins.

5. The weather in the north was cold.

**B.** Write a main idea sentence for each title.

6. A Great American

7. Why History Is Important

8. Problems Americans Have Today

9. What Life Will Be Like in the Future

10. Why I Love My Country

**C.** **Grammar Link** **11.–15.** Write a detail sentence for each main idea sentence from Practice B. Replace some nouns with pronouns.

### Writing Activity    A Paragraph

Write a paragraph about how you solved a problem. State the main idea and use details to support it.
**APPLY GRAMMAR:** Circle each pronoun you use.

# Better Sentences

## Directions

Read the paragraph. Some parts are underlined. The underlined parts may be one of the following:

- Incomplete sentences
- Correctly written sentences that should be combined

Choose the best way to write each underlined part.

*Look for sentences with similar words that can be combined.*

*Check to see if the group of words is a complete sentence.*

> **Sample**
>
> Peter saw a cowboy hat in the store window. <u>It had feathers around the band</u>. <u>It had shiny stones around the band</u>. Peter wanted that hat. Dad said he had to earn the money. Peter took out the trash. He swept the floor. <u>Soon enough money</u>! He raced to the store and paid for the hat. But when he put it on, it fell down over his eyes and nose.
>
> (1) ... (2)

**1**  ○ Band of feathers and shiny stones.

  ○ It had feathers and shiny stones around the band.

  ○ It had feathers. It had shiny stones.

**2**  ○ Enough money!

  ○ Soon he had enough money!

  ○ Soon he had. Enough money!

**Test Tip**
Read the whole paragraph before choosing your answers.

# Vocabulary and Comprehension

## Directions

Read the paragraph. Then read each question that follows the paragraph. Choose the best answer to each question.

---

**Sample**

Long ago there was a big ocean. Dinosaurs walked on the shore of this <u>huge</u> ocean. They left their footprints in the mud. The footprints hardened. The mud turned to stone. Millions of years later people found the footprints. They showed how dinosaurs walked and where they lived. People can learn about dinosaurs by studying their footprints.

---

*See if other words have almost the same meaning as the underlined word.*

**1** In this paragraph, the word <u>huge</u> means—

○ small

○ sandy

○ big

○ shallow

**2** What is the main idea of this paragraph?

○ Long ago there was an ocean.

○ Dinosaurs are very old.

○ People like to see footprints.

○ People can learn about dinosaurs from their footprints.

# Seeing Like a *Writer*

Imagine yourself in these pictures. What ideas for writing do they give you? Think about how you would explain what is happening in each one.

*Mother and Child* by Leslie Braddock.

# Benjamin Franklin

### by Marisa Montez

Benjamin Franklin lived long ago. He was born in Boston in 1706. He went to Philadelphia. There he helped the city set up its library and fire department.

Ben Franklin enjoyed science. He did experiments with electricity. He invented the lightning rod.

Franklin took part in the Revolutionary War. He signed the Declaration of Independence. Later he helped write the Constitution.

Benjamin Franklin died in 1790. He was a great American.

## PRACTICE and APPLY

### Publish Your Own Expository Writing

**1.** Check your revised draft one more time.

**2.** Make a neat final copy. Add a cover.

**3.** Include some pictures of your subject.

## TECHNOLOGY

**Does your school have a web site on the Internet? If so, you may want to publish your work on it.**

# Present Your Expository Writing

**Plan before you present your biography.**

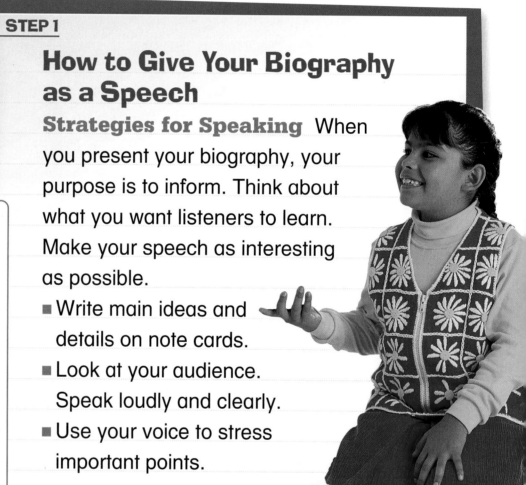

## STEP 1

### How to Give Your Biography as a Speech

**Strategies for Speaking** When you present your biography, your purpose is to inform. Think about what you want listeners to learn. Make your speech as interesting as possible.

- Write main ideas and details on note cards.
- Look at your audience. Speak loudly and clearly.
- Use your voice to stress important points.

### Listening Strategies

- Set a purpose. Why are you listening?

- Listen for main ideas and interesting details.

- Keep your eyes on the speaker.

- Raise your hand to ask questions at the end of the talk.

### Multimedia Ideas

You might want to use sound effects and music you find on the Internet. Tape-record the sounds yourself and play them during the speech.

# How to Show Your Biography

**Suggestions for Illustrations** Pictures can help bring a presentation to life.

- A portrait can help others "see" the person in your biography.
- Maps and drawings can help the audience imagine important events.

# How to Share Your Biography

**Strategies for Rehearsing** It is a good idea to practice before you give a speech.

- Tape-record yourself. Then listen to the tape. How can you improve your presentation?
- Practice in front of a mirror.
- Rehearse in front of family members or a friend. Ask for suggestions.

**Viewing Strategies**

- Study the materials on display.
- Use drawings to help you understand information.
- Look for facts that the speaker does not tell you directly.

## PRACTICE and APPLY

**Present Your Own Expository Writing**

1. Write notes about main ideas and details.

2. Practice your presentation.

3. Vary your tone of voice as you speak.

4. Use pictures and photographs.

5. Add sound effects or music.

# Writing Tests

Read the prompt on a writing test carefully for key words and phrases that tell what to write about and how to do your writing.

*Who will the audience be?*

**Prompt**

Think about all the things that can be done with ice.

Write one or two paragraphs for your teacher that tell things to do with ice. Include facts and details about the ways ice is used.

*Look for words that tell if the purpose of the writing is to inform or entertain.*

*What does this tell you about the kind of writing?*

## How to Read a Prompt

**Purpose** Look for key words in the prompt that tell you the purpose of writing. The words "tell things to do with ice" let you know that one purpose is to inform.

**Audience** The prompt might tell you who the audience is. The words "for your teacher" let you know that your teacher is the audience.

**Expository Writing** The words "facts and details" are clues that this is expository writing. In expository writing, you give information about something. Your writing should have a main idea, and should give facts and details to support the main idea.

**Test Tip**
Read all the parts of a writing test slowly and carefully.

Test Power

## How to Write to a Prompt

Here are some tips to remember when you are given a prompt in a writing test.

| | |
|---|---|
| **Before Writing**<br>**Content/Ideas** | • Think about your writing purpose.<br>• Remember who your audience is.<br>• Make a list of things you know about the topic. |
| **During Writing**<br>**Organization/**<br>**Paragraph**<br>**Structure** | • Start with a good main idea.<br>• Give details about the main idea.<br>• Put your ideas in an order that makes sense.<br>• Give your writing a good ending. |
| **After Writing**<br>**Grammar/Usage** | • Proofread your work.<br>• Use end marks correctly.<br>• Use pronouns correctly. |

## Apply What You Learned

Find words that tell you what to write about. Look for the purpose and the audience. Think about how you will present your ideas.

---

**Prompt**

Think about what you know about whales.

Write one or two paragraphs for your teacher telling what you know about whales. Give details about where they live, what they eat, and what they do.

---

331

# Grammar and Writing Review

pages
280–285,
288–289

## Pronouns and Pronoun-Verb Agreement

**A.** **Write the sentences. Replace the underlined words with a pronoun.**

1. <u>My sister</u> plays the piano.

2. <u>My mother and I</u> sing along.

3. My father claps for <u>Jan, Mom, and me.</u>

pages
290–291

## Possessive Pronouns

**B.** **Write each sentence. Use a possessive pronoun for the underlined words.**

4. <u>My grandfather's</u> stories are interesting.

5. <u>The story's</u> ending was a surprise.

6. <u>My sister's</u> laughter was loud.

pages
292–293

## Contractions: Pronoun and Verb

**C.** **Write each sentence. Use a contraction for the underlined words.**

7. <u>We are</u> going to the play.

8. <u>It is</u> at our school.

9. <u>I am</u> bringing my camera.

page
294

## Mechanics and Usage

**D.** **Write the sentences. Choose the correct contraction or possessive pronoun in ( ).**

10. (Its, It's) a good day to work in the garden.

11. Did you bring (your, you're) tools?

12. Jill and Dan brought (their, they're) rakes.

pages
304–305

## Vocabulary: Synonyms

**E. Write each sentence. Choose the synonym in ( ) for the underlined word.**

**13.** Dance classes <u>begin</u> early. (start, end)

**14.** It seems <u>chilly</u> in this room. (warm, cool)

**15.** My new tap shoes are <u>shiny</u>. (dull, bright)

**16.** New steps are not <u>easy</u>. (simple, hard)

**17.** I feel <u>sleepy</u> after class. (tired, lively)

pages
306–307

## Composition: Main Idea and Details

**F. Write only the sentences that support this main idea: Many countries have folk dances.**

**18.** Step dancing is a favorite in Ireland.

**19.** My brother likes to dance.

**20.** The United States has the square dance.

pages
324–325

## Proofreading a Report

**G. 21.–25. Write the article correctly. There are 5 mistakes.**

Square Dancing

Many people in the United states like to square dance. Its so much fun! You need four pairs of danceers for a square dance. They faces each other in a square.  A caller sings or calls out they're moves.

# Project File

**A Humorous Story**

A **story** tells about made-up characters and events. A funny story entertains readers.

> You will need to know the form of a story when you write your story in the next unit.

## Corky's Mixed-up Morning

Corky Crocodile woke up and smiled. "I have a feeling that today will be a good day!" he said.

First, Corky squeezed the toothpaste tube. All the toothpaste squirted out. There was toothpaste everywhere! "Oh, no!" said Corky. He cleaned up the mess and went to the kitchen.

Next, Corky poured a glass of milk. He dropped the milk carton. There was milk everywhere! "Oh, no!" said Corky. He cleaned up the mess. Then he headed back to his room.

"Where are you going, Corky?" his mother asked.

"I'm going back to bed," said Corky. "My morning started out all wrong. I'd better start over!" With that, he jumped into his bed and then got up again.

*Beginning tells who the story will be about.*

*Middle tells what happens in the story.*

*Time-order words help explain the order of events.*

*End tells how everything turns out.*

**Create a funny story** about something that happened to you or someone else. Or, make up a story from your imagination and use a made-up character as the star. What happened at the beginning? What happened next? What happened at the end?

PROJECT 2

## A Realistic Article

Scientists have been working to save the wolves at Yellowstone. Interview experts at a zoo or search the Internet to find out more about the animals that are in danger of becoming extinct.

**Animals in Trouble**

Choose one group of animals. Write an article about how people are saving these animals.

## Extra Practice

# Pronouns

**A. Write the correct pronoun in ( ) for the underlined words.**

1. <u>A backyard picnic</u> is fun. (It, They)

2. <u>My friends and I</u> had a picnic. (They, We)

3. <u>Felipe and Carmen</u> fixed sandwiches. (You, They)

4. <u>Mario</u> made lemonade. (He, You)

5. <u>Ana</u> peeled some carrots. (They, She)

6. <u>Mom and I</u> baked cookies. (She, We)

7. <u>Dad</u> carried the picnic basket. (We, He)

8. <u>The basket</u> was very heavy. (She, It)

9. <u>Ana</u> spread out the blanket. (They, She)

10. <u>My friends</u> sat on the blanket. (We, They)

**B. Write each sentence. Write pronouns to replace the underlined words.**

11. <u>Peanut butter sandwiches</u> make me thirsty.

12. <u>Carmen</u> poured the lemonade.

13. <u>The lemonade</u> tasted cold and sweet.

14. <u>Felipe and I</u> took some cookies.

15. <u>My dog Charlie</u> snatched a cookie.

# I and Me

**A.** **Write the sentences. Choose _I_ or _me_ to complete each sentence.**

1. My brother and (I, me) like music.

2. Kurt and (I, me) take piano lessons.

3. Mr. Herman teaches Kurt and (I, me).

4. (I, me) always practice after school.

5. Our teacher gave (I, me) a new song to learn.

6. Sometimes (I, me) sing and play at the same time.

7. Mom likes to listen to Ben and (I, me) play.

8. Yesterday (I, me) went to a concert.

9. Mr. Herman gave (I, me) tickets.

10. Dad took Kurt and (I, me) to the concert.

**B.** **Write each sentence. Choose _I_ or _me_ to fill in the blank.**

11. _____ practice an hour a day.

12. Kurt and _____ are in a show.

13. Kurt will play a song with _____.

14. Mom drives Kurt and _____ to our lessons.

15. Kurt and _____ ride home with Dad.

## Extra Practice

# We and Us

**A.** Choose the correct pronoun in ( ) to replace the underlined words. Write the sentence.

1. <u>Lisa and I</u> went to see Mrs. Ruiz. (We, Us)

2. <u>My sister and I</u> brought cookies. (We, Us)

3. Mrs. Ruiz asked <u>Lisa and me</u> to come in. (we, us)

4. She hugged <u>my sister and me</u>. (we, us)

5. Her dog greeted <u>Lisa and me</u>, too. (we, us)

6. <u>Lisa and I</u> patted Pepito. (We, Us)

7. Sometimes <u>she and I</u> walk Pepito. (we, us)

8. <u>My family and I</u> mow the lawn. (We, Us)

9. <u>Mrs. Ruiz and my family</u> are neighbors. (We, Us)

10. Mrs. Ruiz babysat for <u>Lisa and me</u>. (we, us)

**B.** Write each sentence. Write *we* or *us* in place of the underlined words.

11. Mrs. Ruiz made <u>Lisa and me</u> cocoa.

12. <u>Lisa and I</u> served the cookies.

13. Pepito barked at <u>Mrs. Ruiz, Lisa, and me</u>.

14. <u>Mrs. Ruiz, Lisa, and I</u> laughed.

15. <u>Lisa and I</u> gave Pepito a special treat.

# Using *I* and *Me*

**A.** Choose the correct word or words in ( ). Write the sentence.

1. My sister and (i, I) like to bake.

2. Mom gave (Sarah and me, me and Sarah) a cookbook.

3. Sarah and (i, I) checked the recipes.

4. (I and she, She and I) picked one.

5. Mom worked with (Sarah and me, me and Sarah).

6. Sarah, Mom, and (I, me) made bread.

7. (Mom and I, Mom and i) found the bowls.

8. She showed (Sarah and me, me and Sarah) the mixer.

9. (Mom and i, Mom and I) poured the batter.

10. (Sarah and I, Sarah and me) learned how to turn on the oven.

**B.** Write each sentence. Change the sentences that do not use *I* and *me* correctly.

11. Dad asked Sarah and I for a taste of the bread.

12. Mom sliced the bread for me.

13. Sarah and me gave Dad a slice.

14. Dad gave Sarah and I a hug.

15. Sarah and I are good bakers.

# Pronoun-Verb Agreement

**A.** **Write each sentence. Underline the pronoun. Circle the verb.**

1. I like baseball most of all.

2. We play all summer long.

3. I see Max and Yoko.

4. They wait for us at the field.

5. He plays ball all the time.

6. He always brings a bat and ball.

7. She takes her glove everywhere.

8. We still need more players.

9. You call Jack, Ed, and Eli.

10. They live down the block.

**B.** **Choose the correct form of verb in ( ). Then write the sentence.**

11. I (throw, throws) the first pitch to Sara.

12. She (hit, hits) the ball hard.

13. It (land, lands) over the fence.

14. She (send, sends) two runners home.

15. They all (cheer, cheers) for Yoko.

# Possessive Pronouns

**A.** **Write each sentence. Draw a line under each possessive pronoun.**

1. Her class is at the White House.

2. His office and home are here.

3. All of its curtains are new.

4. His mother works for the President.

5. Her office is in the West Wing.

6. Their rooms are private.

7. Their guide leads the way.

8. Her name is Ms. Gomez.

9. Look at its beautiful paintings.

10. Where is her office?

**B.** **Write each sentence. Write a possessive pronoun for the underlined words in the sentence.**

11. The children's friends saw the President.

12. The President's family arrived in Delaware.

13. The First Lady's parents live there.

14. The house's gardens are beautiful.

15. Juan's grandma lives next door.

**Grammar**

## Contractions: Pronoun and Verb

**A.** Write each sentence. Draw a line under each contraction.

1. We're reading a really good book.

2. You're going to like it.

3. It's about a boy and his friends.

4. They're all in the second grade.

5. He's always having adventures.

6. I'm writing a report about the author.

7. She's one of my favorite authors.

8. I'm reading a book by Maurice Sendak.

9. He's another of my favorite authors.

10. You're welcome to read my books.

**B.** Write each sentence. Write the contraction that replaces the underlined words.

11. It is fun to go to the library.

12. I am going there with Jan and Ed.

13. She is looking for books by Tomie de Paola.

14. He is doing a report on the American flag.

15. We are leaving in a few minutes.

# Contractions and Possessive Pronouns

**A.** Choose the correct word in ( ). Then write the sentence.

1. (You're, Your) friends are in science class.

2. (Their, They're) learning about the wind.

3. I read (their, they're) report on storms.

4. (Its, It's) really interesting.

5. (Your, You're) doing a good job, too!

6. (Your, You're) report is great!

7. (Its, It's) steps are easy to follow.

8. (Its, It's) hard to catch raindrops.

9. (Their, They're) not really like teardrops.

10. (Their, They're) shapes are different.

**B.** Write each sentence. Correct the sentence if the underlined word is wrong.

11. <u>Its</u> time to go.

12. <u>Their</u> going to the weather museum.

13. <u>It's</u> my favorite place to visit.

14. <u>Your</u> class will like it.

15. <u>Your</u> going next week.

343

Dry on the inside, wet on the outside. A guest looks out a window.

A hotel worker brings guests' belongings in a waterproof case.

# Write Now!

If you could sleep any place in the world, where would you choose? The desert? The mountains? In space? Imagine that you are in that place. Write to tell about your first night there.

# Parts of a Book

Books have many different parts. The first page of a book is the **title page**. It tells the name of the book and the names of the author and illustrator.

*All About Frogs* ⌐ Title of book
written by Mary Lou Keller ⌐ Author of book
illustrated by Logan Peck ⌐ Illustrator of book

The **table of contents** follows the title page. It lists the name and page number of each chapter in the book. Here is the table of contents of a book called *All About Frogs* by Mary Lou Keller.

*Name of chapter*

**CONTENTS**

*Chapter number*

| Chapter | | Page |
|---|---|---|
| 1 | Frog or Toad?............ | 5 |
| 2 | Frog Eggs............... | 8 |
| 3 | Tadpoles............... | 11 |
| 4 | Grown-up Frogs ......... | 14 |
| 5 | Food for Frogs .......... | 18 |
| 6 | Home for Frogs.......... | 22 |

*Page on which chapter begins*

An **index** is found at the back of most books that give facts. It helps you find information quickly. The index lists in ABC order all the topics in the book and their page numbers.

## Practice

**A. Use the title page and table of contents to answer these questions.**

**1.** What is the title of the book?

**2.** Who is the author?

**3.** How many chapters are in the book?

**4.** What is the name of Chapter 3?

**5.** Which chapter might tell how frogs and toads are alike and different?

**6.** On what page does Chapter 2 begin?

**7.** Which chapter tells about frog eggs?

**8.** Which chapter would you look in to find out what frogs eat?

**9.** On what page would you begin reading about tadpoles?

**10.** What is Chapter 4 about?

**inter NET**
**CONNECTION**

**Go to**
www.mhschool.
com/language-arts

**for more information about parts of a book.**

**Writing Activity**  **A Story**

Write a story about a favorite animal. Use the ideas in your story to make up chapter titles for a book.

# Vocabulary: Antonyms

## DEFINITION

Antonyms are words with opposite meanings.

| | | |
|---|---|---|
| young/old | hot/cold | good/bad |
| tall/short | inside/outside | wild/tame |
| old/new | wet/dry | few/many |
| quiet/noisy | hard/soft | dirty/clean |

**THINK AND WRITE**

**Antonyms**

Write how you can use antonyms to make your writing more interesting.

Look at the blue antonyms below.

*One morning Sam saw some people move into the empty house next door.*

*Sam could see two people talking quietly. One looked old and the other looked young. The old man walked inside. The young boy stayed outside. Sam looked down from his window.*

*Suddenly a bird chirped noisily. The boy looked up. He saw Sam in the window and waved.*

## Practice

**A.** Write the two antonyms in each row.

1. easy     top     small     hard
2. small     day     far     near
3. big     dirty     clean     good
4. tall     short     first     evening
5. right     sad     fine     happy

**B.** Write each sentence. Use an antonym from the box to replace the underlined word.

6. Ned says it is <u>easy</u> to move.
7. The <u>last</u> thing to do is make friends.
8. Sam thinks Ned is <u>mean</u>.
9. The boys become friends <u>slowly</u>
10. Ned is now Sam's <u>worst</u> friend.

| | |
|---|---|
| tidy | loose |
| wet | first |
| best | kind |
| hard | wild |
| high | quickly |

**C.** | Grammar Link | Write each sentence. Write the antonym of each underlined word.

11. The boys do <u>few</u> things together.
12. They play on <u>different</u> teams.
13. Ned is a <u>slow</u> runner.
14. Sam is <u>sad</u> for Ned when Ned wins.
15. Each day they find <u>less</u> to like.

## Writing Activity    A Character Description

Write about someone that you really like. Use at least one pair of antonyms. Choose describing words.

**APPLY GRAMMAR:** Draw a line under each adjective.

# Composition: Beginning, Middle, End

If a writer writes a clear beginning, middle, and end, it is easy to follow what happens.

---
**GUIDELINES**

- The beginning is the start of the story. It describes the characters and the problem.

- The middle tells what happens as the characters try to solve the problem.

- The end is the last part of the story. It tells how the problem gets solved.

---

**THINK AND WRITE**

**Beginning, Middle, End**

Write about why it is important for a story to have a clear beginning, middle, and end.

Read this story. Notice how the writer made the beginning, middle, and end very clear.

*A clear beginning tells about the characters and the problem.*

Millie is a white mouse. She lives in a big cage in Mr. Berg's classroom. Millie has toys and children to play with her, but she is BORED!

*The middle tells what happens.*

Millie plans to run away. When Sam opens the cage to play with her, Millie slips out the door. She hops to the floor and races away.

*In the end, the problem is solved.*

The children chase after Millie. They laugh and try to catch her. Millie is not bored any more.

## Practice

**A.** Write each sentence. Write *beginning, middle,* or *end* to tell where it belongs in the story.

**1.** Annie goes to a pet store to look for a kitten.

**2.** Annie wants a new kitten.

**3.** Annie sees a kitten named Fluff.

**4.** Annie takes Fluff home.

**5.** Annie's mom buys Fluff for her.

**B.** Write beginning sentences for stories with these titles.

**6.** Fuzzy's Haircut

**7.** The Runaway Sled

**8.** A Terrible Sound

**9.** Where's My Bed?

**10.** One Dog Too Many

**C.** **Grammar Link** Use *and* to combine the underlined words. Write the new sentences.

**11.** Sid sits quietly. He sits calmly.

**12.** He wags his long tail. He wags his fluffy tail.

**13.** Sid barks loudly. He barks happily.

**14.** Sid jumps up. He jumps down.

**15.** Sid lets the friendly child pat him. Sid lets the quiet child pat him.

### Writing Activity  A Story Ending

Write an ending for one of the stories you started in Practice B. Check your spelling and punctuation.

**APPLY GRAMMAR:** Use one adjective and one adverb.

# Better Sentences

## Directions

Read the paragraph. Some parts are underlined. The underlined parts may be one of the following:

- Incomplete sentences
- Correctly written sentences that should be combined

Choose the best way to write each underlined part.

*Two sentences with many of the same words can be put together.*

*An incomplete sentence needs to have words added.*

### Sample

Many bears go to sleep in the winter. A mother and her cubs might sleep in a cave.
**(1)**
A mother and her cubs might sleep in a hole. They don't eat much. They eat a lot the rest of the year. Hungry when they wake up in the
**(2)**
spring. That's why people sometimes say, "I'm as hungry as a bear."

**1** ○ A mother and her cubs. Sleep in a cave or in a hole.

○ A mother and her cubs might sleep in a cave or in a hole.

○ A mother. Cubs sleep in a cave.

**2** ○ When they wake up in the spring and are hungry.

○ Hungry when they wake up. It is spring.

○ They are hungry when they wake up in the spring.

**Test Tip**
Remember to read the underlined parts carefully.

# Vocabulary and Comprehension

## Directions

Read the paragraph. Then read each question that follows the paragraph. Choose the best answer to each question.

> **Sample**
>
> Beany was a baby whale. All of Beany's friends were seals. Beany wanted to join the seal games, but he couldn't clap his flippers. He couldn't bark like a seal. Beany sadly turned away.
>
> "The only thing I can do is this," thought Beany, and he blew out a tall stream of water. It sprayed all over the seals. They laughed and splashed and swam with Beany. Now Beany <u>gladly</u> played with his friends.

*Look for a word that is the opposite of the underlined words.*

**1** Name the characters in this story.
- ○ Beany and the mother whale
- ○ Beany and the seals
- ○ seals and friends
- ○ Beany and the whales

**2** What is a word that means the opposite of <u>gladly</u>?
- ○ sadly
- ○ badly
- ○ happily
- ○ loudly

# Seeing Like a Writer

Each of these pictures tells a story. What stories do you see? Tell about the characters in your stories and the problems they have to solve.

*The Hit* by Lance Richbourg.

## Writing from Pictures

1. Make a list of action verbs and adverbs that describe what the children in the pictures are doing.

2. Pick one of these pictures to be on the cover of a book. Write a title for that book.

3. Choose two pictures that could go together in a story. Write what your story would be about.

**Apply Grammar:** Use adjectives and adverbs. Underline each adjective. Circle each adverb.

379

# A Story

A story tells about interesting characters and events. A story can also tell how characters solve their problems.

## Learning from Writers

See how this author writes a clear beginning, middle, and end for his story.

# Swimmy's Escape

A happy school of little fish lived in a corner of the sea somewhere. They were all red. Only one of them was as black as a mussel shell. He swam faster than his brothers and sisters. His name was Swimmy.

One bad day a tuna fish, swift, fierce and very hungry, came darting through the waves. In one gulp he swallowed all the little red fish.

Only Swimmy escaped. He swam away in the deep wet world. He was scared, lonely and very sad.

But the sea was full of wonderful creatures, and as he swam from marvel to marvel Swimmy was happy again.

— Leo Lionni from *Swimmy*

## The Poor Dog

Long ago there was a little dog named Rover. He was a poor dog who had no home. People didn't care. Some children would stop to stare.

Then one day a little boy took Rover home in his arms. Rover's life was good now. He was no longer a poor dog. When he was three he was already famous. He could do many tricks, like flip, play dead, and roll over.

Even though he was famous and loved, he was still just a dog that didn't brag. Rover loved his life.

— Laurie Bennis

## PRACTICE and APPLY

**Thinking Like a Reader**

1. How did Swimmy feel after he escaped?

2. How did you picture Rover as you read "The Poor Dog"?

**Thinking Like a Writer**

3. How did the author show how Swimmy felt?

4. What describing words help you "see" Rover?

5. **Reading Across Texts** Tell why "Swimmy's Escape" and "The Poor Dog" are both fun to read.

# Features of a Story

## DEFINITIONS AND FEATURES

A story tells about made-up characters and what happens to them. A good story does these things:

- ▸ **It entertains** the reader.

- ▸ It has a clear **beginning, middle,** and **end**.

- ▸ It uses **describing words** to tell about its characters, setting, and plot.

### ▸ Entertains

Reread "Swimmy's Escape" by Leo Lionni on page 380. What makes this story fun to read?

> One bad day a tuna fish, swift, fierce and very hungry, came darting through the waves. In one gulp he swallowed all the little red fish.

The author makes the story exciting.

▶ **Beginning, Middle, End**

Each story should have a clear beginning, middle, and end. The beginning introduces the characters and the problem. The middle tells how the characters try to solve the problem. The ending shows how everything turns out.

> But the sea was full of wonderful creatures, and as he swam from marvel to marvel Swimmy was happy again.

How did the author show that Swimmy solved his problem?

▶ **Describing Words: Characters**

To help readers "see" the characters and what they are doing, an author uses adjectives and adverbs. Describing words tell the reader what kind, how many, how, when, and where.

> Only one of them was as black as a mussel shell.

What describing words did the author use?

## PRACTICE and APPLY

**Create a Features Chart**

1. List the features of descriptive writing.

2. Reread "The Poor Dog" by Laurie Bennis on page 381.

3. List the characters and problem in the story.

| Features | Examples |
| --- | --- |
|  |  |

# Prewrite

A story tells about interesting characters and what happens to them as they try to solve their problems.

## Purpose and Audience

The purpose of writing a story is to entertain the reader. Think about who will read your story. Create characters and events that readers will find fun or interesting.

## Choose a Topic

Start by **brainstorming** a list of possible characters and events for your story. Then choose one your readers will like.

**Explore** your ideas **and list**.

### THINK AND WRITE

**Audience**

Write how an audience might tell the difference between a story and expository writing.

*This will be a fun story.*

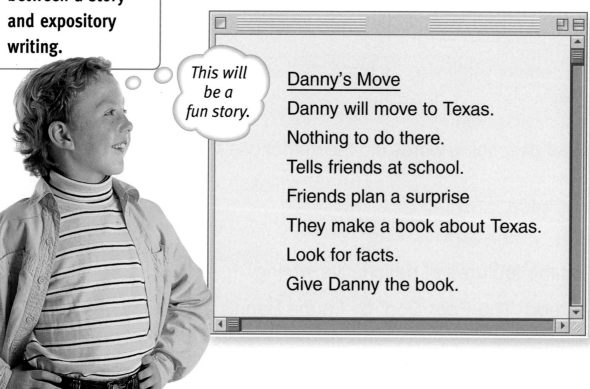

Danny's Move

Danny will move to Texas.

Nothing to do there.

Tells friends at school.

Friends plan a surprise

They make a book about Texas.

Look for facts.

Give Danny the book.

## Organize • Beginning, Middle, End

A good story has a clear beginning, middle, and end. To plan your story, you can use a story map.

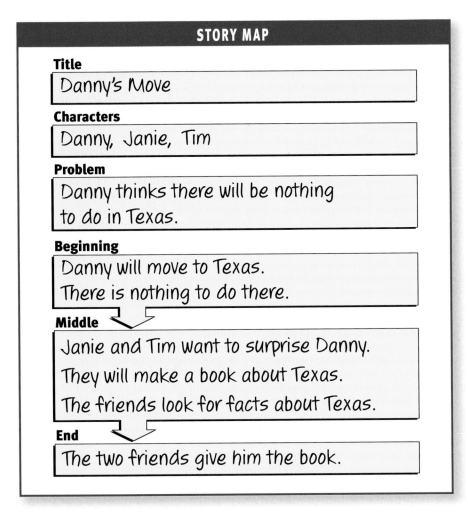

### STORY MAP

**Title**
Danny's Move

**Characters**
Danny, Janie, Tim

**Problem**
Danny thinks there will be nothing to do in Texas.

**Beginning**
Danny will move to Texas.
There is nothing to do there.

**Middle**
Janie and Tim want to surprise Danny.
They will make a book about Texas.
The friends look for facts about Texas.

**End**
The two friends give him the book.

## Checklist ✓

**Prewriting**

■ Did you brainstorm story ideas?

■ Did you think about your purpose and audience?

■ Does your story have a clear beginning, middle, and end?

■ Do you need to find out any more information?

## PRACTICE and APPLY

**Plan Your Own Story**

1. Brainstorm story ideas.

2. Choose a character, or characters, and something that will happen.

3. Plan the story's beginning, middle, and end.

**Writing** PROCESS

# Prewrite • Research and Inquiry

## ▶ Writer's Resources

To make your story seem real, you may need to do some research. Start with a list of questions. Then find resources to answer them.

| What Else Do I Need to Know? | Where Can I Find the Information? |
|---|---|
| Are there interesting facts about Texas? | Look in the card catalog at the library for a book about Texas. |
| What fun things are there to do in Texas? | Look at chapter titles in books about Texas. |

## ▶ Card Catalog

A card catalog lists all the books in a library. You can look up books by title, author, or subject. Some catalogs are online.

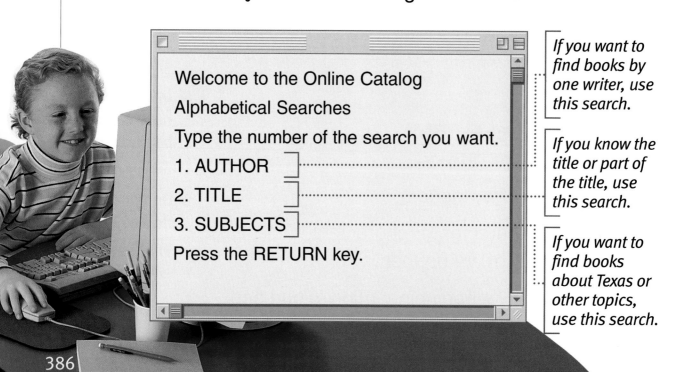

Welcome to the Online Catalog

Alphabetical Searches

Type the number of the search you want.

1. AUTHOR
2. TITLE
3. SUBJECTS

Press the RETURN key.

If you want to find books by one writer, use this search.

If you know the title or part of the title, use this search.

If you want to find books about Texas or other topics, use this search.

# A Surprise for Danny
by James Clay

PREWRITE

DRAFT

REVISE

PROOFREAD

PUBLISH

This summer Danny will move to Texas. Danny thinks there is nothing to do there.

Tim and Janie plan a special surprise for Danny. They will make a book about fun things to do in Texas. The friends look in the library to learn more about Texas. Janie and Tim read A Texas Tour for Kids. They read about the Dallas World Aquarium. It is the largest freshwater aquarium in the world. Danny has always wanted to visit an aquarium.

The next week Danny's kind friends give him the book they made. Danny hugs his book and smiles.

## PRACTICE and APPLY
### Publish Your Own Story

1. Read your story again.

2. Copy your story neatly.

3. Add drawings or pictures.

4. Put your story in a class book of stories.

## TiP!

### Handwriting

Take your time and write your story neatly. Try leaving a little extra space between each line. That will help to make your writing easy to read.

395

# Present Your Story

**Planning ahead will make your presentation better.**

## Listening Strategies

- Think about why you are listening. Will you learn something new? Is it just for fun?

- Try to picture the characters and events.

- Look at the speaker. Show that you are enjoying the story.

- Listen to the speaker's voice. See if it changes at different parts of the story.

**STEP 1**

## How to Tell Your Original Story

**Strategies for Speaking** When you tell a story, you are like an actor. Be a storyteller and have fun.

- Highlight important words on note cards.
- Look your audience in the eye.
- If the story is exciting, make your voice sound excited. If a character in the story is happy, smile as you speak.
- Speak loudly and clearly.

## Multimedia Ideas

You might want to tape-record music to play with your story while you tell it. Ask a librarian to help you find the music.

# How to Show Your Original Story

**Suggestions for Illustrations** Show pictures to get your audience interested.

- Draw the characters or events.
- Cut out pictures of people from magazines who could be your characters and paste them on poster board.
- Label your pictures.

# How to Share Your Original Story

**Strategies for Rehearsing** Be sure to practice your story ahead of time.

- Tell your story to a partner.
- Tell your story to family members.
- If you make a mistake, just keep going.

## PRACTICE and APPLY

**Rehearse Your Own Story**

1. Write note cards to help you remember.

2. Collect the things you will show.

3. Practice telling the story so you know it well.

4. Ask a friend to listen to you practice.

**TiP!**

## Viewing Strategies

- Look at the drawings or objects the speaker shows.

- Read the labels.

- Use the drawings to learn more about the characters or events than the speaker tells you.

# Writing Tests

Remember to read the prompt on a writing test carefully. Look for key words and phrases that tell you what to write about and how to do your writing.

*Sometimes a prompt does not tell who the audience is.*

*Look for words that tell the purpose of the writing.*

*Look for words that tell you the kind of writing to do.*

> **Prompt**
>
> One day two friends were looking in a toy chest. What they saw surprised them.
>
> <u>Write a story</u> telling all about <u>what the two friends saw</u> and <u>what happened</u>.

## How to Read a Prompt

**Purpose**   Look at the prompt again. Find the words that tell you the purpose of the writing. The words "write a story" tell you that the purpose will be to entertain.

**Audience**   If the prompt does not name the audience, you can think of your teacher as your audience.

**Writing a Story**   When you write a story, you tell about characters and how they solve a problem. The words "what they saw surprised them" lets you know something unusual is about to happen. The words "what the two friends saw" and "what happened" tell you that the story should have a beginning, middle, and end.

**Test Tip**
Remember to plan your writing before you begin doing it.

398

## How to Write to a Prompt

Remember these tips when you are given a writing prompt.

| | |
|---|---|
| **Before Writing**<br><br>Content/Ideas | • Think about your writing purpose.<br>• Remember who your audience is.<br>• Plan the beginning, middle, and ending of your story. |
| **During Writing**<br><br>Organization/<br>Paragraph<br>Structure | • Start with a good opening sentence.<br>• When writing a story, use describing words to tell about characters.<br>• Tell what happens in the story.<br>• Give the story a good ending. |
| **After Writing**<br><br>Grammar/Usage | • Proofread your work.<br>• Begin each sentence with a capital letter.<br>• Spell each word correctly.<br>• Make sure adjectives and adverbs are used correctly. |

## Apply What You Learned

Find words that tell what the writing will be about. Think about the purpose and audience. Plan your writing. Put the events in order.

> **Prompt**
>
> Imagine that you saw a dinosaur and wanted it for a pet.
> Write a story telling what happened when you took the dinosaur home.

## Grammar and Writing Review

pages
346–353
### Adjectives and Articles

**A.** Write the sentences. Choose the correct word in ( ). Underline each adjective.

**1.** Pip is (a, an) tiny pig.

**2.** Pip is the (smaller, smallest) pig on the farm.

**3.** Once (a, an) angry bee stung Pip's nose.

pages
356–361
### Adverbs

**B.** Write the sentences. Underline each adverb. Circle the verb it describes. Write if the adverb tells *how*, *when*, or *where*.

**4.** Amy quickly walks to the library.

**5.** Amy goes upstairs to the children's room.

**6.** Soon Amy finds a book about Mars.

pages
354, 362
### Mechanics and Usage: Book Titles and Quotation Marks

**C.** Write the sentences. Use quotation marks correctly. Use capital letters and underline words correctly.

**7.** My favorite book is lemonade for sale, I said.

**8.** Jan asked, Have you read strega nona?

**9.** The same author wrote the popcorn book, Jan said.

pages
372–373

### Vocabulary: Antonyms

**D. Write each sentence. Circle the antonym in ( ) for the underlined word.**

10. The gray kitten is <u>cute</u>. (ugly, pretty)

11. <u>Little</u> kittens are a lot of fun. (small, big)

12. The kittens are <u>rough</u> with each other. (gentle, playful)

pages
374–375

### Composition: Beginning, Middle, End

**E. Write 1, 2, and 3. Put the sentences in an order that makes sense. They should tell a story that has a beginning, a middle, and an end.**

13. As soon as I fell asleep, I was a robot!

14. I went to bed after watching a movie about robots.

15. I heard my mother say, "Wake up, Eric," and I knew it had all been a dream.

pages
392–393

### Proofreading a Story

**F. 16.–20. Write the story correctly. There are 5 mistakes.**

Kayla's Big Adventure
    At bedtime, Kayla and her mother red a story called <u>Where the Wild things Are</u>. Soon Kayla fell asleep Then a amazing thing happened. She became part of the story.
    The next morning, Kayla woke up and said, What a great adventure that was!"

# Project File

## PROJECT 1  A Poem

A **poem** paints a picture with words.

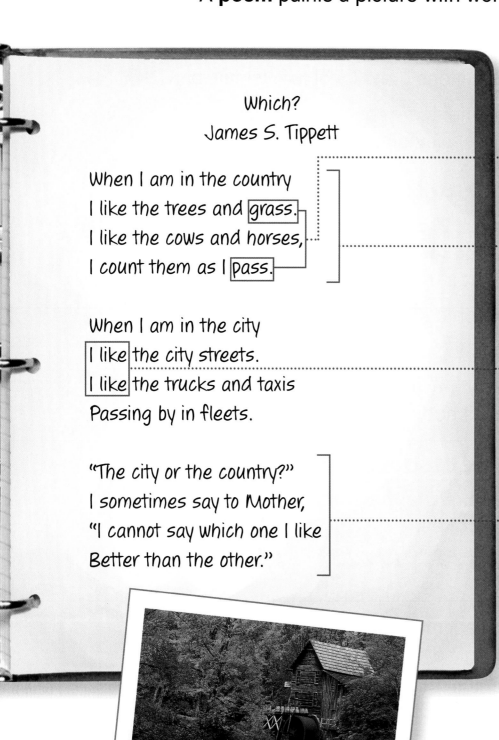

Which?

James S. Tippett

When I am in the country
I like the trees and grass.
I like the cows and horses,
I count them as I pass.

When I am in the city
I like the city streets.
I like the trucks and taxis
Passing by in fleets.

"The city or the country?"
I sometimes say to Mother,
"I cannot say which one I like
Better than the other."

**Rhyme** *Some poems have words that rhyme, or share the same ending sound.*

**Rhythm** *We say that a poem has rhythm when it has a set beat from line to line.*

**Repeated words** *A poet may repeat words to add rhythm or stress an idea.*

**Form** *Poems can take different forms. This poem has three parts of four lines each. Each part is called a stanza.*

**Make up a poem** about clouds. Look out the window. Are there any clouds in the sky? What shapes are they? What do the clouds look like to you? Choose a cloud and draw an outline of it. If you don't see a cloud, imagine one.

Write a poem. Will your poem rhyme? Will your poem have rhythm? What describing words will you choose? Write your poem inside the cloud shape you drew.

**PROJECT 2**

## A Point of View

How would you like to stay in an underwater hotel like the one in Florida? What must the fish think as they look at you through the round windows?

**A Fish-Eye View** Write an imaginary conversation between two fish. What are they saying about the people in the underwater hotel?

## Extra Practice

## Adjectives

**A.** **Write each sentence. Circle the adjective that describes each underlined noun.**

1. This year we had a different <u>Thanksgiving</u>.

2. After dinner, Dad took me to the funny <u>parade</u> in town.

3. We stood on a crowded <u>curb</u>.

4. The bands played loud <u>marches</u>.

5. Marchers wore colorful <u>costumes</u>.

6. A silly <u>clown</u> shook my hand.

7. Riders on white <u>horses</u> waved.

8. I liked the big <u>floats</u>.

9. Dad bought me hot <u>cocoa</u>.

10. Instead of walking home, we decided to take the new <u>bus</u>.

**B.** **Write each sentence. Circle the adjective or adjectives.**

11. We had a great dinner.

12. Dad carved the golden turkey.

13. Mom made tasty stuffing and hot gravy.

14. We also had green beans and red beets.

15. Grandma made creamy pies for dessert.

# Adjectives That Tell *How Many*

**A.** Write each sentence. Circle the adjective that tells *how many*.

1. I bought one watermelon.

2. It weighed nine pounds.

3. It cost three dollars.

4. I gave the clerk five dollars.

5. The clerk gave me two dollars back.

6. Dad cut the melon into four parts.

7. Each part had many seeds.

8. I counted fifty seeds in my part.

9. I planted ten seeds.

10. I soon had ten plants.

**B.** Write each sentence. Fill in the blank with an adjective that tells *how many*.

11. Mom bought ＿＿＿ tomatoes.

12. Dad wanted ＿＿＿ grapes and peaches.

13. My sister didn't want ＿＿＿ melon.

14. We spent ＿＿＿ dollars at the market.

15. We grew ＿＿＿ vegetables.

## Extra Practice

### Articles: *a, an*

**A.** **Choose the correct article in ( ).**
**Write each sentence.**

**1.** My sister is writing (a, an) story.

**2.** Her story is about (a, an) ox.

**3.** The ox lives on (a, an) island.

**4.** The island is in (a, an) ocean.

**5.** The ox goes on (a, an) adventure.

**6.** The ox meets (a, an) butterfly on the way.

**7.** The two friends follow (a, an) path.

**8.** The path leads to (a, an) forest.

**9.** The ox and the butterfly meet (a, an) owl.

**10.** The story doesn't have (a, an) ending yet.

**B.** **Write each sentence. Fill in the blank with**
**the correct article.**

**11.** I have _____ book of animal stories.

**12.** My favorite story is about _____ eagle.

**13.** The eagle has never seen _____ airplane.

**14.** One day _____ jet flies over the eagle's nest.

**15.** "What kind of _____ bird are you?" he asks.

## Adjectives That Compare

**A.** **Choose the correct adjective in ( ). Write each sentence.**

1. My seeds grew the (faster, fastest) of all.

2. Now your plants are (taller, tallest) than mine.

3. Pedro's plants are (smaller, smallest) than Hillary's.

4. Hillary's plants are the (taller, tallest) so far.

5. Her plants have the (thicker, thickest) stems.

6. Those roots are the (longer, longest) of all.

7. My plants are the (smaller, smallest) here.

8. Your soil feels (damper, dampest) than mine.

9. Hillary's soil is the (damper, dampest) in the room.

10. These leaves are (greener, greenest) than the others.

**B.** **Write each sentence. Add *-er* or *-est* to each word in ( ).**

11. Our garden is the (small) one around.

12. The cucumbers are the (long) ever.

13. Some peppers are (green) than others.

14. The corn is (tall) than the tomato plants.

15. Our spinach grew the (fast) of all.

## Grammar

# Writing Book Titles

**A.** Write each book title using capital letters where they belong.

1. digging up dinosaurs
2. johnny appleseed
3. fire! fire!
4. the post office book
5. koko's kitten
6. the maple tree
7. see through the forest
8. a duckling is born
9. dancing masks of africa
10. song of the swallows

**B.** Write each sentence. Use capital letters where they belong. Underline the words in the title of each book.

11. My favorite book is henry and mudge.
12. The last book I read was wagon wheels.
13. I want to read sam the minuteman.
14. My cousin just read hill of fire.
15. Did you enjoy reading a very young rider?

## Adverbs

**A.** Write *how*, *when*, or *where* for the underlined adverb in each sentence.

1. <u>Yesterday</u> I saw a baby rabbit.

2. I was <u>outside</u> in the yard.

3. I tiptoed <u>quietly</u> to look.

4. I kneeled <u>down</u>.

5. <u>Then</u>, I called for my mom.

6. She was <u>upstairs</u>.

7. Mom <u>quickly</u> found a carrot.

8. We walked <u>softly</u> across the yard.

9. Mom put the carrot <u>down</u>.

10. We went back <u>inside</u> the house.

**B.** Write each sentence. Underline the adverb. Then write *how, when,* or *where* to tell about the adverb.

11. The rabbit hopped slowly to the carrot.

12. The rabbit smelled the carrot carefully.

13. Then the rabbit took a bite!

14. It crunched the carrot loudly.

15. Mom and I watched happily.

## Extra Practice

# Adverbs That Tell *How*

**A.** **Write each sentence. Circle the adverb that tells *how* the underlined action is done.**

1. Dad and I <u>walk</u> slowly to the tank.

2. We <u>watch</u> the fish quietly.

3. One fish <u>watches</u> us closely.

4. It <u>clings</u> tightly to the tank glass.

5. The fish suddenly <u>moves</u>.

6. It <u>swims</u> quickly to a rock.

7. Another fish <u>glides</u> by smoothly.

8. Seaweed <u>sways</u> gently in the tank.

9. Some pretty stones <u>shine</u> brightly there.

10. The whole tank really <u>interests</u> me!

**B.** **Write each sentence. Underline each verb. Circle each adverb that tells *how*.**

11. Dad and I happily watch the dolphin show.

12. Two dolphins swim playfully.

13. The trainer whistles loudly.

14. How swiftly the dolphins come!

15. The dolphins jump easily.

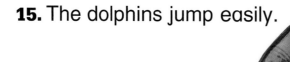

# Adverbs That Tell *When* or *Where*

**A.** **Write each sentence. Circle the adverb that tells about the underlined verb. Then write *when* or *where* for each adverb.**

1. Yesterday we <u>started</u> our vacation.

2. Our car <u>pulled</u> away at six o'clock.

3. We <u>stopped</u> nearby for gas.

4. Afterward Dad <u>drove</u> to the highway.

5. Then the car <u>got</u> a flat tire.

6. Our family <u>didn't drive</u> far!

7. Dad soon <u>changed</u> the tire.

8. We <u>stopped</u> later for lunch.

9. Mom, Dad, and I <u>sat</u> outside.

10. Mom and I <u>walked</u> around.

**B.** **Write each sentence. Underline each verb. Circle each adverb and write *when* or *where*.**

11. Today we hiked in the mountains.

12. We walked up.

13. Dad and I walked ahead.

14. Mom stopped often to take photos.

15. We returned to camp early.

411

**Grammar**

# Quotation Marks

**A.** Write each sentence that has quotation marks. Circle the words that a person says.

1. "Are you ready?" asked Mom.

2. I asked, "Where are we going?"

3. "Did you forget?" asked Mia.

4. Mia said she was going to the dentist.

5. Dad told Mia to brush her teeth.

6. "Don't forget to floss," Dad added.

7. Mom called, "We'll be in the car."

8. Mia asked us to hurry up.

9. "We can't be late," she said.

10. "I'm coming now," I answered.

**B.** Write each sentence. Add quotation marks where they belong.

**11.** Who's next? the nurse said.

**12.** I'm next, answered Kristen.

**13.** The nurse said, Come with me.

**14.** Okay, Kristen said to the nurse.

**15.** Have a seat, said Dr. Soo.

**16.** Have you been brushing? asked Dr. Soo.

**17.** Yes, answered Kristen.

**18.** Your teeth look very nice, said Dr. Soo.

**19.** Thank you, said Kristen.

**20.** You should be proud, said Dr. Soo.

# Cumulative Review

**Unit 1** **Sentences**

**A. Begin and end each sentence correctly. Write the sentence.**

1. my mom, dad, and I visited friends

2. what a great time we had

3. tell us all about it

4. what did you do

5. we went to the beach

**B. Combine each pair of sentences with _and_. Underline the subject in the new sentence.**

6. Al joined the team. Tina joined the team.

7. Ann ran quickly. Ted ran quickly.

8. My sister raced ahead. I raced ahead.

9. Dad watched. Our coach watched.

10. Mom cheered for us. Grandma cheered for us.

**Unit 2** **Nouns**

**A. Write the sentences. Circle each noun.**

11. The family goes to the park.

12. The children are happy.

13. The baby sits in the swing.

14. The girls go down the slide.

15. The dog barks at the squirrels.

**B.** Write each sentence. Capitalize proper nouns.

**16.** Today is tuesday, october 4.

**17.** The elm street children's club meets today.

**18.** My friends amy and jeff are coming.

**19.** We are in the columbus day parade.

**20.** We have practice on saturday.

## Unit 3  Verbs

**A.** Write each sentence. Use the correct verb in ( ).

**21.** Jon T. Dean, Jr., (write, writes) books.

**22.** My friends and I (like, likes) his books.

**23.** I (have, has) his last two books.

**24.** Amy (wish, wishes) for the latest book.

**25.** Mr. Dean's books (make, makes) us laugh.

**B.** Use *and* to combine the underlined predicates. Write the new sentence.

**26.** Connie loves birds. Connie reads about robins.

**27.** Robins like people. Robins live in open places.

**28.** The female bird builds the nest. The female bird lays blue eggs.

**29.** Robins like fruit. Robins eat insects, too.

**30.** Their songs fill the air. Their songs sound cheerful.

**Grammar**

**Unit 4** **Verbs and Punctuation**

**A.** **Write the correct verb in ( ). Then write *linking verb* or *helping verb*.**

31. We (are, have) worked hard all day.

32. Now I (am, was) very hungry.

33. Mom and Dad (are, have) fixing dinner.

34. I'll do homework after I (am, have) eaten.

35. Dinner (is, were) ready at last!

**B.** **Change the underlined verbs to the past tense. Write the sentence.**

36. I <u>see</u> Amanda and <u>run</u> to meet her.

37. Amanda <u>says</u>, "Let's do something."

38. We <u>go</u> home and <u>do</u> homework first.

39. Dad <u>comes</u> home and <u>gives</u> us a new CD.

40. Amanda and I <u>sing</u> along.

**C.** **Write each sentence. Add apostrophes and commas where they belong.**

41. Moms new job is in Dallas Texas.

42. My sister and I arent very happy.

43. We dont want to leave Tulsa Oklahoma.

44. The Lee twins grandmother lives there.

45. They say that Dallas isnt so far.

**Pronouns**

**A.** Write each sentence. Replace the underlined words with the correct pronoun. Choose the correct verb.

**46.** <u>Ann and Jim Smith</u> (live, lives) in a small town.

**47.** <u>Ann's and Jim's</u> mom (work, works) in an office.

**48.** <u>Mrs. Smith's</u> job (is, are) in the city.

**49.** <u>Mrs. Smith</u> (take, takes) the train.

**50.** <u>The train</u> (come, comes) every half hour.

**B.** Write each sentence. Replace the underlined words with the correct contraction.

**51.** <u>I am</u> very lucky!

**52.** <u>We are</u> going to a nice place.

**53.** <u>It is</u> called Bryce Canyon.

**54.** <u>We are</u> meeting with Mr. and Mrs. Berg.

**55.** <u>They are</u> park rangers there.

**C.** Write each sentence. Use the correct pronoun in ( ).

**56.** My brother and (I, me) don't like to go to bed early.

**57.** We always ask Dad to read (we, us) a story.

**58.** (We, Us) have many favorite books.

**59.** After the story, Dad tells Patrick and (I, me) to close our eyes.

**60.** (I, Me) often start to giggle.

**Unit 6** **Adjectives, Adverbs, and Quotation Marks**

**A.** Write each sentence. Underline the adjective. Circle the adverb. Write if it tells *how, when,* or *where.*

**61.** Tonight Dad read a new story.

**62.** He sat down in the old rocker.

**63.** Dad slowly opened the big book.

**64.** The two boys listened eagerly.

**65.** Soon the sleepy children began yawning.

**B.** Write each sentence. Choose the correct article or adjective in ( ). Add quotation marks where needed. Use capital letters correctly in the book titles.

**66.** Lori said, Here's (a, an) interesting book called elephants of africa .

**67.** Are elephants the (larger, largest) land animals? Juan asked.

**68.** Cal said, My book called big trunks says that (a, an) African elephant is very large.

**69.** Lori added, It is (larger, largest) than the Asian elephant.

**70.** Juan said to himself, What (a, an) beautiful animal it is!

# Troubleshooter

## Contents

# Incomplete Sentences

- A **sentence** is a group of words that tells a complete thought.

- An **incomplete** sentence does not tell a complete thought.

## Problem 1

**An incomplete sentence that does not have a predicate**

Incomplete Sentence: *My best friend.*

> What about my best friend?

### Solution 1

**What is** or **what happens** is called the **predicate** of the sentence. You must add a predicate to this incomplete sentence to make it a complete sentence.

Complete Sentence: *My best friend plays on my team.*

## Problem 2

**An incomplete sentence that does not have a subject**

Incomplete Sentence: *Warm up first.*

> Who warms up first?

### Solution 2

**Who** or **what** is called the **subject** of the sentence. You must add a subject to this incomplete sentence to make it a complete sentence.

Complete Sentence: *We warm up first.*

**Troubleshooter**

## Problem 3

**An incomplete sentence that does not have a subject or a predicate**

Incomplete Sentence: *At ten o'clock.*

> Who is this about? What happened?

### Solution 3

You must add a subject and a predicate to this incomplete sentence to make it a complete sentence.

Complete Sentence: *Our soccer game starts at ten o'clock.*

**Practice** Write the incomplete sentences correctly. Add a subject, a predicate, or a subject and a predicate.

1. The game is over. Wins the first match.

2. The coaches smile. Proud of us.

3. Both teams line up. All the players.

4. I run to Mom and Dad. A big hug.

5. I like soccer. A great sport.

 **Need More Help?** For more help, see Subjects in Sentences on pages 10–11, Predicates in Sentences on pages 12–13, and Handbook page 433.

# Confusing Plurals and Possessives

- A plural noun names more than one person, place, or thing.

- A possessive noun shows who or what owns or has something. A possessive noun needs an apostrophe.

## Problem 1

**Using an apostrophe in a plural noun**

Incorrect: *The kitten's are so cute.*

> Is more than one kitten cute?

### Solution 1

A plural noun does not need an apostrophe (').

Correct: *The kittens are so cute.*

## Problem 2

**Leaving out the apostrophe in a singular possessive noun**

Incorrect: *The dogs name is Spike.*

> How do you show that the name belongs to one dog?

### Solution 2

You need to add an apostrophe (') and *-s* to a singular noun to make it possessive.

Correct: *The dog's name is Spike.*

## Problem 3

**Leaving out the apostrophe in a plural possessive noun**

Incorrect: *The horses names are Rocket and Jet.*

> How do you show that the names belong to two horses?

### Solution 3

A **plural possessive noun** shows what more than one person, place, or thing has. You need to add an **apostrophe** (') to most plural nouns to make them possessive.

Correct: *The horses' names are Rocket and Jet.*

**Practice** Write the sentences correctly. Add apostrophes that are needed. Take out apostrophes that are not needed.

1. Birds make good pets. My two sister's have pet birds.

2. My sisters' birds are small. The birds cages are big.

3. Parakeets are cute. Both bird's are parakeets.

4. Ann's bird has blue feathers. Amys bird is green.

5. Some birds talk. Both girls' have birds that talk.

**Need More Help?**

For more help, see Plural Nouns on pages 78–79, Singular Possessive Nouns on pages 82–83, Plural Possessive Nouns on pages 84–85, and Handbook pages 436–437.

# Lack of Subject-Verb Agreement

- In a sentence, a present-tense verb must be singular if the subject is singular.

- Do not add *-s* or *-es* to a present-tense verb that tells about more than one person or thing.

## Problem 1

**Using a plural verb with a singular subject**

Incorrect: *Jack take notes.*

> Is the subject one or more than one?

### Solution 1

You need to add *-s* or *-es* to the present-tense verb to make the verb and the subject agree.

Correct: *Jack takes notes.*

## Problem 2

**Using a singular verb with a plural subject or *I* or *you***

Incorrect: *The girls adds trees and grass.*

> How do you make the verb agree with its subject?

### Solution 2

When the subject of a sentence is more than one person or thing or *I* or *you*, do not add *-s* or *-es* to a present-tense verb.

Correct: *The girls add trees and grass.*

## Problem 3

**Using a singular verb when a subject has two nouns joined by *and***

Incorrect: *Sam and Lisa draws cars.*

How many nouns are in the subject?

### Solution 3

When the subject of a sentence has two nouns joined by *and*, you do not add *-s* or *-es* to a present-tense verb. Take out *-s* or *-es* to make the subject and verb agree.

Correct: *Sam and Lisa draw cars.*

**Practice Write the sentences correctly. Make the subject and verb agree.**

1. Everyone cleans up. Miss Jones help us.

2. Jen and Tina gather the brushes. Ted and Al washes them.

3. I put away the scissors. You closes the jar of paste.

4. The boys study the mural. The girls looks, too.

5. You say, "What a great mural!" I likes it a lot.

For more help, see Present-Tense Verbs on pages 142–143, Subject-Verb Agreement on pages 144–145, and Handbook pages 438–439.

425

# Incorrect Verb Forms

- The verbs *have* and *be* have special forms in the present tense and in the past tense.

- Some verbs do not add *-ed* in the past tense.

- An apostrophe (') takes the place of the letters that are left out when two words are combined.

## Problem 1

**Using the incorrect form of *be* or *have***

Incorrect Form of *be*: *We is going to the pond today.*

> What present-tense form of *be* goes with *We*?

### Solution 1

You need to use the form of *have* or *be* that agrees with the subject of the sentence and helps show the action.

Correct Form of *be*: *We are going to the pond today.*

## Problem 2

**Forming the past tense of irregular verbs incorrectly**

Incorrect Form of Irregular Verb:
*I runned all the way home.*

> What is the past form of *run —* *runned* or *ran*?

### Solution 2

You need to use the special forms of the irregular verbs.

Correct Form of Irregular Verb: *I ran all the way home.*

426

## Problem 3

**Leaving out the apostrophe in a contraction**

Incorrect Contraction:

*Our town doesnt have an ice rink.*

What takes the place of the left-out letter in *doesnt*?

### Solution 3

A **contraction** is a short form of two words.
You need to add an apostrophe (') to take the place of the letters that are left out.

Correct Contraction: *Our town doesn't have an ice rink.*

**Practice** **Write the sentences. Be sure to write each verb correctly.**

1. Mom is coming to the pond. We were leaving now.

2. I have skated for two years. Mom have helped me a lot.

3. Mom did a spin for me. I gived it a try.

4. The spin isn't so easy. I didnt get dizzy.

5. My friends saw me. They sayed, "Good for you!"

**Need More Help?** For more help, see Helping Verbs on pages 212–213, Irregular Verbs on pages 218–223, Contractions with *not* on pages 224–225, and Handbook pages 440–441.

**Troubleshooter**

427

# Incorrect Use of Pronouns

- Use *I* and *me* to tell about yourself.

- Use *we* and *us* to tell about yourself and another person.

- Some contractions and possessive pronouns sound alike.

## Problem 1

**Using *me* or *us* as the subject**

> Incorrect: *Dad, Ben, and me fix breakfast.*

> *Which sounds right: "I fix" or "me fix"?*

## Solution 1

Do not use *me* or *us* as the subject of a sentence. Use the pronouns *I* or *we* instead.

> Correct: *Dad, Ben, and I fix breakfast.*

## Problem 2

**Using *I* or *we* in the predicate**

> Incorrect: *Officer Lee helps we cross the street.*

> *Where does we come—before the verb or after it?*

## Solution 2

Use the pronouns *me* or *us* after an action verb.

> Correct: *Officer Lee helps us cross the street.*

428

## Problem 3

### Confusing contractions and possessive pronouns

Using a Contraction for a Possessive Pronoun: *Please take you're seat.*

> Can you say "You are seat"?

### Solution 3

A possessive pronoun shows who or what owns something. A pronoun-verb contraction is a shortened form of a pronoun and a verb. It has an apostrophe.

Using a Possessive Pronoun Correctly: *Please take your seat.*

**Practice** Write the sentences. Be sure to write all pronouns, contractions, or possessive pronouns correctly.

**1.** Ben and I study. Tomorrow he and me have a test.

**2.** Mom helps Ben and me. She gives him and I a problem.

**3.** It's not so hard. Its really easy.

**4.** Mom said, "You're ready. You're brother is ready, too."

 For more help, see *I* and *Me* on pages 282–283, *We* and *Us* on pages 284–285, Possessive Pronouns on pages 290–291, Contractions—Pronoun and Verb on pages 292–293, and Handbook pages 442–443.

# Incorrect Use of Adjectives

- You can use adjectives to compare people, places, and things.

- Add *-er* to an adjective when you compare two nouns.

- Add *-est* to an adjective to compare more than two nouns.

## Problem 1

**Using *-er* or *-est* incorrectly**

Incorrect: *Our pine tree is tallest than our oak tree.*

*Are you comparing two or more than two?*

### Solution 1

Count how many people, places, or things you are comparing. Then add *-er* or *-est*.

Correct: *Our pine tree is taller than our oak tree.*

**Practice** Write each sentence. Be sure to write adjectives that compare correctly.

1. Toads have shorter back legs than frogs. Frogs have smoothest skin than toads.

2. What is the world's longest fish? The whale shark is the longer fish of all.

3. Lions are faster than zebras. Are zebras fastest than rabbits?

4. The ostrich is the largest bird of all. The hummingbird is the smaller bird of all.

# Handbook

# Contents

**Handbook**

**RULE 1**
pages 2–3

## Sentences

- A sentence tells a complete thought. Words that do not tell a complete thought are not a sentence.

**Practice** **Write each complete sentence.**

1. Blackie is a gerbil.

2. He runs on his wheel.

3. Is very small and furry.

4. Our teacher and the students.

5. Dina touches his fur.

**RULE 2**
pages 4–5, 6–7

## Kinds of Sentences

- Every sentence begins with a capital letter.

| Kind of Sentence | Example |
| --- | --- |
| A statement tells something. It ends with a period. | *Firefighters put out fires.* |
| A question asks something. It ends with a question mark. | *Why do firefighters wear boots?* |
| A command tells someone to do something. It ends with a period. | *Watch the firefighters climb the ladder.* |
| An exclamation shows strong feeling. It ends with an exclamation mark. | *At last, the fire is out!* |

**Practice** **Tell what kind of sentence you see.**

1. Firefighters work together.

2. Would you like to be a firefighter?

3. What a great job it is!

**Handbook**

---

### Names and Titles of People

- The names of people begin with a capital letter.

  *Martha Bates*        *Jason S. Golov*

- Titles begin with a capital letter.

  *Senator Hunter*     *Aunt Terri*     *Mr. Wasserman*

- Always make the pronoun *I* a *capital letter*.

  *My sister Natalie and I went apple picking.*

---

**Practice**  **Write the sentences. Use capital letters correctly.**

**1.** We visited mr. cook's apple orchard.

**2.** Natalie and i picked lots of apples.

**3.** We watched mrs. cook make apple cider.

---

### Names of Places

- The names of cities, states, countries, and continents begin with a capital letter.

  *Chicago    Nevada    Canada    Africa*

- The names of streets, buildings, and planets begin with a capital letter.

  *Longwood Street*     *Lincoln Memorial*     *Earth*

---

**Practice**  **Write the sentences. Use capital letters correctly.**

**1.** Erica visited her best friend Katie in england.

**2.** Katie lives on dexter street in london.

**3.** They saw a famous clock called big ben.

**Handbook**

### More Proper Nouns and Adjectives

- The names of schools, clubs, and businesses begin with a capital letter.

  *Ambrose School   Drama Club   Randal Company*

- The days of the week, months of the year, and holidays begin with a capital letter. Do not begin the names of the seasons with a capital letter.

  *Sunday        June        Columbus Day        winter*

- Most abbreviations have capital letters.

  *Dr.        Ms.        St.        Mt.*

- The first, last, and all important words in the title of a book, poem, song, story, play, movie, magazine, and newspaper begin with a capital letter.

  *The Owl and the Pussycat*
  *The Wizard of Oz*
  *The Los Angeles Times*

**Practice** Write the sentences. Use capital letters correctly.

1. Julie's class at rockville school is having a science show.

2. Julie is in the young inventors club.

3. The science show is this spring in may.

4. It's on memorial day at the b & k arena.

5. The *rockville news* is printing a story about the science show.

**Handbook**

## End Marks

- A statement is a sentence that tells something. It ends with a period (.).

  *We have a birdfeeder in our backyard.*

- A command is a sentence that tells or asks someone to do something. It ends with a period (.).

  *Buy some seeds for the birds.*

- A question is a sentence that asks something. It ends with a question mark (?).

  *Do they like sunflower seeds?*

- An exclamation is a sentence that shows strong feeling. It ends with an exclamation mark (!).

  *That bag of seeds is too big!*

## Periods

- Use a period to show the end of an abbreviation. An abbreviation is the short form for a word.

  *Mr.    Dr.    Ave.*

- Use a period with initials. Initials are capital letters that stand for a person's name.

  *J. P. Morgan    C. S. Lewis*

**Practice  Write the sentences. Add end marks.**

1. Lots of sparrows come to our birdfeeder

2. Don't make loud noises near the birdfeeder

3. How many birds do you count

4. There are so many birds

**Handbook**

---
**Commas**
---

- Use a comma (,) between the names of cities and states.

  *Seattle, Washington     Detroit, Michigan*

- Use a comma between the day and the year in dates.

  *December 25, 2001     July 4, 1776*

- Use a comma after the greeting and closing in a letter.

  *Dear Grandpa,     Sincerely,*

**Practice** Write the items. Add commas.

**1.** Orlando Florida

**2.** April 1 2002

**3.** Your best friend

**4.** Dear Aunt Betty

---
**Commas**
---

- Use a comma to separate words in a series.

  *Jeremy plays soccer, t-ball, and hockey.*

- Use a comma after the words *yes* or *no* or the name of a person being spoken to.

  *Yes, he likes soccer. Jim, do you play tennis?*

**Practice** Write the sentences. Add commas.

**1.** Marcia do you have a snack for the game?

**2.** Yes I have oranges apples and juice.

**3.** Reynaldo do you want to come to the game?

**4.** No I'm going to my cousin's house.

## Apostrophes

- Use an apostrophe (') with nouns to show possession.

  *girl's drums     Paul's flute     children's music instruments' cases     musicians' chairs*

- Use an apostrophe (') in contractions to show where a letter or letters are missing.

  *doesn't     I'm     we're     can't*

**Practice** **Write the sentences. Add apostrophes.**

**1.** Music is Ginas favorite subject.

**2.** She plays the drums at our schools recitals.

**3.** She doesnt play any other instrument.

## Quotation Marks

- Use quotation marks at the beginning and at the end of the exact words a person says.

  *"Did you do your homework?" asked Mom.*
  *Joseph said, "I'm doing it now."*

## Italics (Underlining)

- Underline or use italics for the title of a book, movie, magazine, or newspaper.

  <u>James and the Giant Peach</u>     *Mary Poppins*

**Practice** **Write the sentences. Add quotation marks or underlines where they are needed.**

**1.** Do you need help with your homework? asked Mom.

**2.** I have to write about a movie, Joseph answered.

**3.** Joseph's brother said, I like Star Wars!

**Handbook**

# Dictionary

── **DEFINITIONS** AND **FEATURES** ──

- A dictionary is a book that tells what words mean.

- Entry words are the words the dictionary tells about. They are in ABC order.

- A sample sentence shows how the word is used.

- The two guide words at the top of each page tell the first and last words on the page.

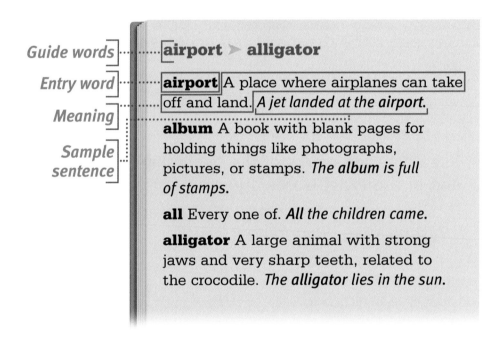

Guide words ········ **airport** ▶ **alligator**

Entry word ········ **airport** A place where airplanes can take off and land. *A jet landed at the airport.*

Meaning ········

Sample sentence ····

**album** A book with blank pages for holding things like photographs, pictures, or stamps. *The album is full of stamps.*

**all** Every one of. *All the children came.*

**alligator** A large animal with strong jaws and very sharp teeth, related to the crocodile. *The alligator lies in the sun.*

**Practice** Use the dictionary page above to answer these questions.

**1.** What are the two guide words on this page?

**2.** Which guide word tells the first word on the page?

**3.** Which guide word tells the last word on the page?

**4.** What is the sample sentence for *all*?

**5.** What does the word *airport* mean?

# Note-taking and Summarizing

## DEFINITIONS AND FEATURES

- When you read paragraphs for information, you can take notes about important ideas.

- You can use your notes to write a summary. A summary tells in a few words or sentences what the paragraph is about.

### Flying Penguins — Underwater

Most people say that penguins can't fly. It is true that they can't fly through the air. However, penguins do fly—underwater! Penguins flap their wings, pushing against water like birds push against air. Air is thin. So most birds have wide, soft wings. Water is dense and heavy. So penguins have short, hardened wings.

Notes
fly through water
flap their wings
push against water
water dense, heavy
short, hardened wings

Summary
Penguins fly underwater, flapping their wings. They have short, hardened wings that help them push against the dense, heavy water.

**Practice** Read the paragraph, the notes, and the summary. Answer these questions.

1. What is the paragraph about?

2. What is the main idea of the paragraph?

3. How are penguins' wings different from birds' wings?

4. Why do penguins need short, hardened wings?

5. Why is the summary shorter than the article?

Handbook

**Handbook**

# Library

---
### DEFINITIONS AND FEATURES
---

- A library has books, newspapers, magazines, and other material on many subjects.

- Fiction books are imagined stories. They are arranged in ABC order by the author's last name.

- Nonfiction books are true. They have facts about real people, places, and things. Nonfiction books are grouped by topic.

- A library also has magazines and newspapers. These are kept in the periodicals section.

- Dictionaries, encyclopedias, and other reference books are kept in the reference section.

- The library media center has videos, tapes, computers, CDs, and CD-ROMs.

**Practice Write the answers to these questions.**

1. Where in the library would you find copies of the magazine *Cricket*?

2. Where would you look for a video of *Charlie and the Chocolate Factory*?

3. Would you find a book with facts about the moon in the fiction or the nonfiction section?

4. Where would you find a make-believe story about the moon?

5. In what section would you find a dictionary?

# Periodicals

---
**DEFINITIONS AND FEATURES**
---

- Magazines and newspapers are called periodicals.

- Magazines often cover many topics. Some magazines are about just one topic. Magazines may come out once a week or once a month.

- Newspapers have facts about events. Most newspapers come out every day.

**Practice** Look at the newspaper and magazine covers. Think about the kind of information you could find in each. Write the name of the one that might give you the following information.

1. a parade in Franklin

2. new stamps

3. paintings of animals

4. easy lunch tips

5. "Caring for Your New Kitten"

Handbook

# Map, Atlas

┌─── **DEFINITIONS** AND **FEATURES** ───────────────

- **Maps** help you find places.

- A map has pictures on it called **symbols**. The **key** tells what the symbols mean.

- An **atlas** is a book of maps.

└────────────────────────────────────────────

**Greenport Zoo**

**Key**

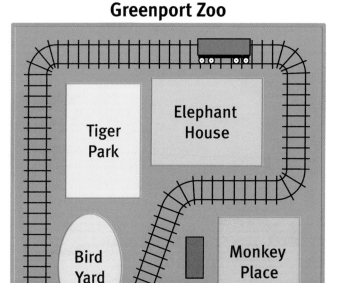

Entrance

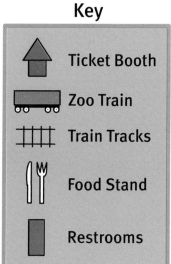

**Practice Use the map to answer these questions.**

**1.** How many symbols are shown on the map?

**2.** What does the symbol [🚃] stand for?

**3.** What animal areas do the train tracks go past?

**4.** What is at the Entrance?

**5.** What animal area is near the Food Stand and the Restrooms?

**Handbook**

**Handbook**

# Telephone Directory

## DEFINITIONS AND FEATURES

- The telephone directory is a list of names, addresses, and telephone numbers.

- The White Pages list the names of people and companies in ABC order.

- The Yellow Pages list different kinds of businesses. Within each group, businesses are listed in ABC order.

- Emergency numbers for police, ambulance, and fire department are found at the front of the telephone directory.

- Guide words at the top of each page give the first and last names on the page.

---

Riley—Rivera

Riley, Michelle
  11 Leonard St., Leeds 555-1814
Rios, Luis Antonio
  134 College Hwy., Holyoke 555-6359
Ripka's Farm
  222 Maple St., S. Deerfield 555-3316

---

**COMPUTERS**

Advanced Computers
  168 Main St., Northfield 555-3742
Mountain Micro
  391 West St., Farmington 555-5875

---

**Practice** Use the directory entries above to answer the following questions.

1. What is Luis Rios's telephone number?

2. What is the address of Mountain Micro?

3. What is the telephone number for Advanced Computers?

4. What is the address of Ripka's Farm?

5. What number would you call to reach M. Riley?

Handbook

# Encyclopedia (CD-ROM)

┌─ **DEFINITIONS** AND **FEATURES** ──────────

- An encyclopedia CD-ROM contains all the information in a set of encyclopedias on a computer disk.

- The Search command can help you find information on your topic.

- Search for your topic by typing in a key word. Some CD-ROMs give you a list of articles from which to choose. Select the article that looks best for your topic.

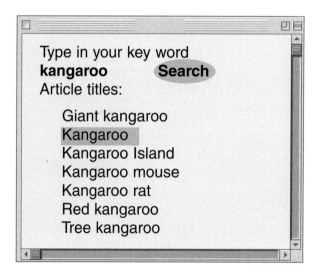

**Practice** Use the computer screen to answer these questions.

**1.** What key word did the person type in?

**2.** How many entries are there for that key word?

**3.** Which article would probably be the best for a report about kangaroos?

**4.** Which articles have information about different types of kangaroos?

**5.** Which articles are probably not about kangaroos?

460

# Diagrams

┌─── **DEFINITIONS** AND **FEATURES** ───

- A diagram is a special kind of drawing. It can show how something is put together or how it works.

- The title tells what the diagram shows.

- Labels name the different parts of the diagram.

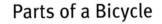
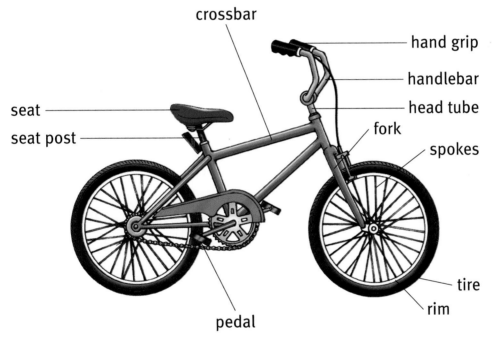

Parts of a Bicycle

crossbar

hand grip

handlebar

head tube

seat

seat post

fork

spokes

tire

rim

pedal

**Practice** Use the diagram to answer these questions.

**1.** What is the title of the diagram?

**2.** What parts make up the wheel of the bike?

**3.** What parts are on the ends of the handlebar?

**4.** What part is between the seat post and the head tube?

**5.** What is the part that holds the front wheel called?

# Alphabetical Order

## DEFINITIONS AND FEATURES

- You can put words in ABC order by their first letter.

- When words begin with the same letter, use the second letter to put them in ABC order.

- When words begin with the same two letters, use the third letter to put them in ABC order.

| ABC Order by Second Letter | ABC Order by Third Letter |
|---|---|
| bank | milk |
| bird | mine |
| black | miss |

**Practice** Write each group of words in ABC order. Use the first, second, or third letter as needed.

1. yellow, blue, orange

2. balloon, butterfly, beaver

3. home, holly, hoe

4. giant, garden, geese

5. milk, music, moon

6. farm, fast, fall

7. jacket, juice, jelly

8. troop, train, truck

9. tomato, thick, tulip

10. write, wing, worm

# Index

**Handbook**

```
┌─ DEFINITIONS AND FEATURES ──────────────────┐
│                                              │
│  • An index lists all the subjects in a book.│
│                                              │
│  • The subjects are listed in ABC order.     │
│                                              │
│  • Each main subject may have one or more subtopics. │
│                                              │
└──────────────────────────────────────────────┘
```

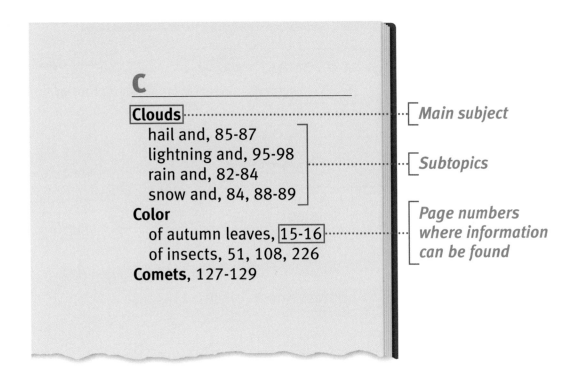

**Practice** Use the index above to answer these questions.

1. What is the first main subject under the letter C?

2. What are the subtopics under Color?

3. How many pages tell about the color of insects?

4. What pages have information on lightning and clouds?

5. On what pages would you find out about comets?

**Handbook**

# Parts of a Book

---
**DEFINITIONS AND FEATURES**
---

- The first page in every book is the title page. It tells the name of the book and the author.

- The table of contents follows the title page. It lists the name and page number of each chapter in the book.

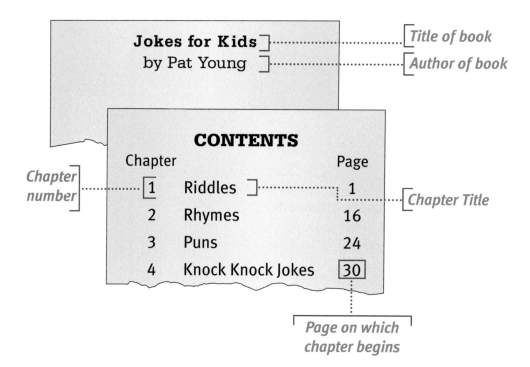

Jokes for Kids ⌉ ···········  ⌈Title of book
by Pat Young ⌉ ···········  ⌈Author of book

### CONTENTS

| Chapter | | Page |
|---|---|---|
| 1 | Riddles | 1 |
| 2 | Rhymes | 16 |
| 3 | Puns | 24 |
| 4 | Knock Knock Jokes | 30 |

Chapter number ······  ⌈Chapter Title

⌈Page on which chapter begins⌉

**Practice** Use the title page and table of contents to answer these questions.

**1.** What is the title of the book?

**2.** What is the author's name?

**3.** What is the title of Chapter 1?

**4.** On what page does Chapter 2 begin?

**5.** What is the number of the chapter on Knock Knock Jokes?

# Card Catalog

## DEFINITIONS AND FEATURES

- The card catalog contains information about all of the books in the library.

- Each book has a title card, an author card, and a subject card.

- The call number helps you find the book.

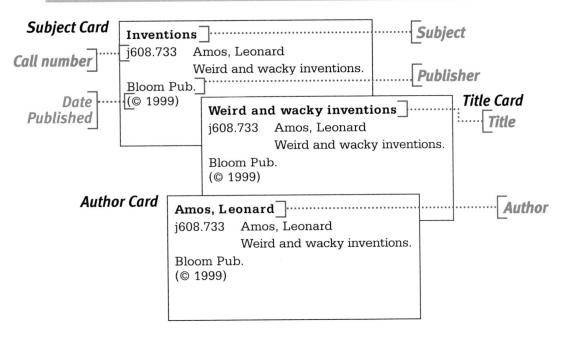

**Practice** Use the catalog cards above to help you answer these questions.

1. If you wanted to find a book on inventions, what card would you use?

2. If you were looking for a book by Leonard Amos, what card would you use?

3. If you knew the book's title but not its author, what card would you use?

4. What is the title of Leonard Amos's book?

5. What is the call number of the book?

**Handbook**

### RULE 1
pages 26–27

## Time-Order Words

- **Time-order words** show the order in which things happen.

- Time-order words help you tell about events in order.

**Time-Order Words and Phrases**

| | | |
|---|---|---|
| first | after | a long time ago |
| next | before | last of all |
| then | later | now |
| last | yesterday | next month |

### RULE 2
pages 96–97

## Compound Words

- A **compound word** is a word that is made from two smaller words.

- Knowing the **meaning** of the two smaller words can help you figure out the meaning of the compound word.

| Two Words | Compound Word | Meaning |
|---|---|---|
| note + book | notebook | a book you take notes in |
| blue + berry | blueberry | a berry that is blue |
| dog + house | doghouse | a house for a dog |
| bed + room | bedroom | a room with a bed in it |

**Handbook**

**RULE 3**
pages
164–165

## Prefixes

- A prefix is a word part that is added to the beginning of a word.

- A prefix changes the meaning of a word.

- You can use prefixes to say things in a shorter way.

| Prefix | Meaning | Example |
|--------|---------|---------|
| un- | not, do the opposite of | unlock |
| re- | again, back | refill |
| dis- | not, the opposite of | disappear |
| pre- | before | preschool |

**RULE 4**
pages
236–237

## Suffixes

- A suffix is a word part that is added to the end of a word.

- A suffix changes the meaning of the word.

| Suffix | Meaning | Example |
|--------|---------|---------|
| -less | without | careless |
| -ful | full of | careful |
| -er | person who | catcher |
| -ly | in a certain way | carefully |

## Vocabulary

**RULE 5**
pages 304–305

### Synonyms

- A **synonym** is a word that has the same or almost the same meaning as another word.

- A synonym can be used instead of another word.

| Word | Synonyms | |
|------|----------|---|
| fast | quick | rapid |
| end | finish | complete |
| little | tiny | small |
| big | huge | giant |
| glad | happy | joyful |
| laugh | chuckle | giggle |
| say | speak | tell |
| see | watch | view |
| cure | heal | fix |
| clean | pure | clear |
| grab | grip | hold |
| true | real | right |

Handbook

**Handbook**

**RULE 6**
pages
372–373

## Antonyms

• **Antonyms** are words with opposite meanings.

| Word | Antonyms | |
|---|---|---|
| young | old | aged |
| tall | short | low |
| old | new | fresh |
| large | small | tiny |
| quiet | noisy | loud |
| happy | sad | unhappy |
| hot | cold | icy |
| dry | wet | damp |
| slow | fast | quick |
| go | stop | halt |
| fly | fall | sink |
| break | fix | repair |

Handbook

## Problem Words

Some words in the English language are confusing. Sometimes these words are not used correctly. The following charts will help you see how to use these words in the correct way.

| Words | Correct Usage | Correct Usage |
|-------|---------------|---------------|
| can/may | *Can* means "to be able to." *My dog* can *run very fast.* | *May* means "to be allowed." *May* we go to the *movies this afternoon?* |
| good/well | *Good* is an adjective that describes a noun. *I am having a* good *day.* | *Well* is often an adverb. *Well* describes a verb by telling "how." *Rena did very* well *on the math test.* |
| in/into | *In* means "inside of." *The bird is* in *the cage.* | *Into* means "move to the inside of." *I stepped* into *the car.* |
| its/it's | *Its* is a possessive pronoun. *Its* has no apostrophe. *The cat likes* its *new toy.* | *It's* is a contraction. It is the shortened form of "it is." *It's* hot outside! |
| lay/lie | *Lay* means "to put something down." *I will* lay *my coat on the chair.* | *Lie* means "to rest on something" *I like to* lie *on my bed and read a book.* |

470

**Handbook**

| Words | Correct Usage | Correct Usage |
|-------|---------------|---------------|
| sit/set | *Sit* means "to be seated." *The teacher asked us to sit in a circle.* | *Set* means to "put something in a certain place." *I set the cup on the saucer.* |
| their/they're | *Their* is a possessive pronoun. It means "belonging to them." *That is their house.* | *They're* is a contraction. It is the shortened form of "they are." *They're going on a field trip tomorrow.* |
| then/than | *Then* means "next." *I walked home from school and then I ate a snack.* | *Than* means "to compare something." *Your dog is bigger than my dog.* |
| to/too | *To* means "in the direction of." *She walked to the door and opened it.* | *Too* is an adverb. It means "also." *I want a pizza, too.* |
| your/you're | *Your* is a possessive pronoun. It means "belonging to you." *Is that your backpack?* | *You're* is a contraction. It is the shortened form of "you are." *I think you're a great friend.* |

**QUICK WRITE** Create your own chart of problem words. Include words from this chart or other words you sometimes get confused. Write sentences to help you remember how to use the words correctly.

471

## Spelling

### Difficult Words to Spell

For many writers, some words are difficult to spell. You can use this list to check your spelling. You can also practice spelling these words correctly.

| | | | | | |
|---|---|---|---|---|---|
| again | been | early | money | said | tired |
| along | before | family | myself | school | together |
| also | buy | finally | o'clock | soon | until |
| always | charge | first | off | started | upon |
| another | clothes | friend | once | sure | were |
| any | color | heard | our | than | when |
| anything | could | hurt | please | their | which |
| around | dear | know | pretty | they | while |
| balloon | decide | little | really | third | would |
| because | does | might | right | through | write |

### Homophones

Homophones are words that sound the same. But they are spelled differently, and they have different meanings. **See** and *sea* are examples of homophones.

| | | | | | |
|---|---|---|---|---|---|
| ant | buy | hear | know | sea | whole |
| aunt | by | here | no | see | hole |
| bare | dear | hour | meat | some | wood |
| bear | deer | our | meet | sum | would |
| be | eye | knew | one | their | to |
| bee | I | new | won | there | too |
| blew | flour | knot | road | threw | two |
| blue | flower | not | rode | through | |

**Handbook**

## Words You Often Use

Here is a list of words that writers often use in their writing. Test yourself and see how many of these words you can spell correctly.

| | | | | | |
|---|---|---|---|---|---|
| a | came | have | me | saw | upon |
| about | can | he | men | say | us |
| after | color | her | morning | school | very |
| all | could | him | mother | see | want |
| am | day | his | my | she | was |
| an | did | home | night | so | we |
| and | didn't | house | no | some | well |
| are | do | I | not | soon | went |
| around | don't | if | now | stand | were |
| as | down | in | of | that | what |
| at | eat | into | on | the | when |
| away | find | is | one | them | where |
| back | first | it | or | then | white |
| ball | for | just | our | there | who |
| be | found | know | out | they | will |
| because | four | last | over | things | wish |
| big | friend | left | people | think | with |
| black | from | like | play | this | woman |
| book | get | little | pretty | time | women |
| box | girl | live | put | to | would |
| bring | go | look | red | too | year |
| but | got | made | run | two | you |
| by | had | man | said | up | your |

Handbook

473

### Spelling Rules and Strategies

Learning these spelling rules can help you spell many words.

1. When words end in silent **e,** drop the **e** when adding an ending that begins with a vowel. **(save + ed = saved)**

2. When a base word ends with a consonant followed by **y,** change the **y** to **i** when adding the ending. **(story + es = stories)**

3. When a base word ends with a vowel followed by **y,** do not change the ending when adding suffixes or endings. **(day = days)**

4. When a one-syllable word ends in one vowel followed by one consonant, double the consonant before adding an ending that begins with a vowel. **(run + ing = running; drop + ed = dropped)**

5. The letter **q** is always followed by **u. (quick)**

6. No English words end in **j, q,** or **v.**

7. Add **-s** to most words to form plurals or to change the tense of verbs. Add **-es** to words ending in **x, z, s, sh,** or **ch. (map = maps; bus = buses; wish = wishes; fox = foxes)**

Use these tips to help you become a better speller.

1. Learn about sound-alike words such as **hear** and **here.** Be sure you use the right one.

2. Use spell-check on a computer. Spell-checkers are not perfect! If you write a word that sounds like the word you need, spell-check will not catch the mistake.

3. Think of a word that rhymes with the new word. Rhyming words often have the same spelling pattern. *(b + and = band; h + and = hand)*

4. Use words you know how to spell to help spell new words. Word beginnings and endings can help. *(<u>st</u>ar + <u>b</u><u>one</u> = <u>st</u><u>one</u>)*

5. Make up clues to help you remember the spelling. *("What you <u>k</u>now is O<u>K</u>." <u>K</u> begins <u>k</u>now.)*

6. Break the word into word parts or syllables. *(be cause)*

7. Look for a smaller word in a new word to help you write the new word. *(<u>heard</u> has <u>hear</u> in it)*

8. Word families have words with the same endings. Use word families to help you spell new words. *(pen, ten)*

9. Use the dictionary to look up spellings of words.

10. Study each letter in words that do not match spelling patterns or rules. Say and write the words carefully.

11. Think of when you have seen the word before. Think of how it looked. Write the word in different ways to see which one looks correct. *(~~fal~~, ~~faul~~, fall)*

12. Keep a Personal Word List in your Spelling Journal. Write words you have trouble spelling.

# Handbook

## Play

A **play** is a story that is written to be acted out. Characters use actions and words, called dialogue, to tell the story.

*A play has a title*

**Jack and the Beanstalk**

*A play has a cast of characters*

Characters: JACK
MOTHER
TESSY THE COW
OLD MAN
GIANT

*The setting tells where and when the play takes place.*

**Setting:** Long ago in a small village

*An act is one part of a play*

**Act I**

**Scene I:** The play begins in Jack's house. Jack and his mother are sitting near an empty fireplace. Tessy is chewing Mother's straw hat.

*A character's words are written after his or her name.*

MOTHER (grabbing her hat away from Tessy) You must sell the cow, Jack, so we can buy something to eat.

JACK No, Mother, Tessy is the only friend I have.

TESSY (nodding her head) Moo.

JACK But, Mother…

MOTHER Don't you "but, Mother" me. The cow goes or I go.

*Stage directions in ( ) tell how the characters move and act.*

TESSY (pushing Mother out of the door) Moooo!

MOTHER Get this cow away from me!

**Practice Think of characters from a story you like. Think about what they do and say. Then write the beginning of the story as a play.**

# Poem

In a **poem**, words are used in special ways to help you imagine an idea or a subject. A poem is different from other writing. It has a special sound and form.

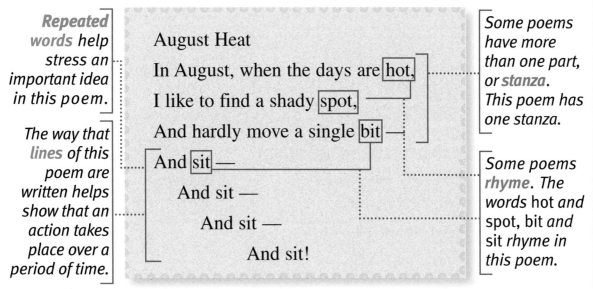

*Repeated words help stress an important idea in this poem.*

*The way that lines of this poem are written helps show that an action takes place over a period of time.*

August Heat
In August, when the days are hot,
I like to find a shady spot,
And hardly move a single bit —
And sit —
   And sit —
      And sit —
         And sit!

*Some poems have more than one part, or stanza. This poem has one stanza.*

*Some poems rhyme. The words hot and spot, bit and sit rhyme in this poem.*

## GUIDELINES FOR WRITING A POEM

- Choose a fun or interesting object or idea.

- Write words that make a picture of the object or idea.

- Do you want your poem to rhyme? Do you want an idea to repeat? Use rhyming words or repeated words in your poem.

- How many stanzas will your poem have? Write as many stanzas and lines as you want.

- Give your poem a title.

**Practice** Look around your classroom or outside. Choose an object or an idea to write a poem about. Then write the poem and draw a picture to go with it.

**Handbook**

# Business Letter

A **business letter** is a special kind of letter. It is more formal than a friendly letter. You can write a business letter to a company or to a person.

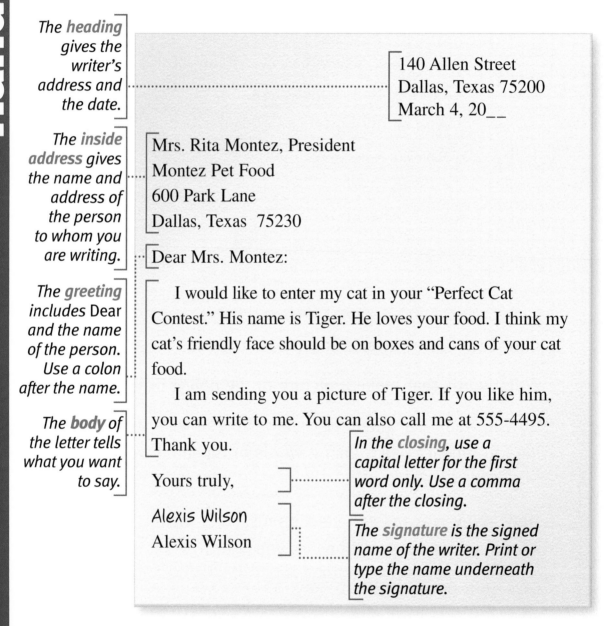

*The **heading** gives the writer's address and the date.*

140 Allen Street
Dallas, Texas 75200
March 4, 20__

*The **inside address** gives the name and address of the person to whom you are writing.*

Mrs. Rita Montez, President
Montez Pet Food
600 Park Lane
Dallas, Texas  75230

*The **greeting** includes Dear and the name of the person. Use a colon after the name.*

Dear Mrs. Montez:

*The **body** of the letter tells what you want to say.*

I would like to enter my cat in your "Perfect Cat Contest." His name is Tiger. He loves your food. I think my cat's friendly face should be on boxes and cans of your cat food.

I am sending you a picture of Tiger. If you like him, you can write to me. You can also call me at 555-4495. Thank you.

Yours truly,

*In the **closing**, use a capital letter for the first word only. Use a comma after the closing.*

Alexis Wilson
Alexis Wilson

*The **signature** is the signed name of the writer. Print or type the name underneath the signature.*

**Practice** Think of something you like about your school. Write a business letter to your principal.

**Handbook**

# Research Report

A **research report** gives information about a subject. You find facts for the report from sources such as encyclopedias, books, magazines, and the Internet.

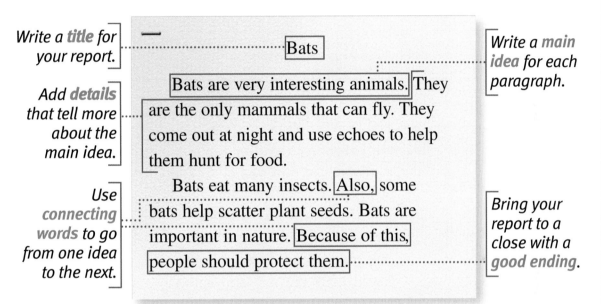

*Write a title for your report.*

*Add details that tell more about the main idea.*

*Use connecting words to go from one idea to the next.*

Bats

Bats are very interesting animals. They are the only mammals that can fly. They come out at night and use echoes to help them hunt for food.

Bats eat many insects. Also, some bats help scatter plant seeds. Bats are important in nature. Because of this, people should protect them.

*Write a main idea for each paragraph.*

*Bring your report to a close with a good ending.*

---

## GUIDELINES FOR WRITING A REPORT

- Choose a topic that you find interesting.

- List questions you have about the topic.

- Do research. Use different sources. You may need to go to the library.

- Take notes on index cards.

- List your sources at the end of your report.

---

**Practice** What topic do you want to learn more about? Write a research report about that topic. Share your report with the class.

# Using the Dictionary

A dictionary is an alphabetical list of words with their meanings and information about how to use them. Look at this entry for *little*.

**Guide words** are found at the top of each page. They tell the first and last entry words on a page.

**Entry words** are the words explained in the dictionary.

**Example sentence** shows how to use a word.

**Antonyms** are words with opposite meanings.

**Syllable division** shows how a word can be divided into smaller parts.

**Definition** is the meaning of a word.

**Synonyms** have the same or almost the same meaning as the entry word.

**Part of speech** tells how a word works in a sentence.

**Pronunciation** respelling shows how a word is spoken.

-less ▶ near

**-less** A suffix that means:
1. Having no; without: *Fearless means having no fear.*
2. That cannot be: *Countless means that cannot be counted.*

**little** 1. Small in size or amount: *A pebble is a little stone.*
2. A small amount: *I wasn't hungry, so I ate only a little.*
**SYNONYMS:** small, tiny;
**ANTONYMS:** big, huge, large.
**lit•tle** (LIHT uhl) *adjective, noun.*

**lucky** 1. Having or bringing good luck: *That lucky boy won first prize.*
2. Caused by good luck: *Maria's home run was a lucky hit.*
**luck•y** (LUK ee) *adjective,*
**luckier, luckiest.**

Dictionary

480

**Practice: Use the example on page 480 to answer these questions.**

1. What are the guide words?

2. What is the first meaning given for *little*?

3. What is the example sentence for the second definition of *little*?

4. What are the synonyms for *little*?

5. Which of these words would come on the same page with the guide words *happy/late*?
   hard, lucky, kind, hot, little

**Practice: Use the dictionary to answer the questions below.**

6. What antonyms are given for *cold*?

7. What synonyms are given for *happy*?

8. Is *quiet* an antonym or a synonym for *noisy*?

9. What two synonyms are listed for *wet*?

10. What are two antonyms for *begin*?

11. How many word parts, or syllables, does *sunflower* have?

12. What is the definition of *blueberry*?

13. What part of speech is the word *lucky*?

14. Does the *a* in *tall* stand for the same sound as in *father* or in *saw*?

15. Which two parts of speech are shown for the word *first*?

When you write a poem, choose words that will paint a clear picture for the reader.

**Practice:** Read the poem below. Use the dictionary to answer the questions.

### Frog on a Log in the Fog

Once I saw a small, sleepy frog

Sitting on a crisp, narrow log.

The frog croaked loudly.

The log went "Crack!"

And all I saw was the cold, dull fog.

**1.** What are the guide words for *small* and *sleepy*?

**2.** What is the definition for *crisp*?

**3.** How many word parts, or syllables, are in *narrow*?

**4.** Which definition of *dull* tells how it is used here?

**5.** What part of speech is the word *narrow?*

# Pronunciation Key

The **Pronunciation Key** has examples for the sound spellings in the **pronunciation** of each dictionary entry. Use the key when you look up how to say a word.

| Sound Spellings | Examples | Sound Spellings | Examples |
|---|---|---|---|
| a | cat | oh | go, home |
| ah | father | oo | too, do |
| air | there, hair | or | more, four |
| aw | saw, fall | ow | out, cow |
| ay | late, day | oy | toy |
| b | bit, rabbit | p | pig |
| ch | chin | r | run, carry |
| d | dog | s | song, mess |
| e | met | sh | shout, fish |
| ee | he, see | t | ten, better |
| f | fine, off | th | thin |
| g | go, bag, bigger | thh | them |
| h | hat | u | sun |
| hw | wheel | û | look, should |
| ih | sit | uh | about, happen, lemon |
| i | fine, tiger, my | ur | turn, learn |
| ihr | near, deer, here | v | very, of |
| j | jump, page | w | we |
| k | cat, back | y | yes |
| l | line, hill | yoo | music, new |
| m | mine, hammer | z | has, zoo |
| n | nice, funny | zh | treasure, division |
| ng | sing | | |
| o | top | | |

**Dictionary**

**A**

**after** Following in place; behind: *My dog followed after.* Adverb.
▲ Following in time; later: *She got there after you left.* Preposition.
**af•ter** (AF tuhr) *adverb; preposition.*

**B**

**backyard** A yard behind a building: *We planted flowers in our backyard.*

**back•yard** (bak YAHRD) *noun, plural* **backyards**.

**bad 1.** Not good: *a bad movie.* **2.** Having a harmful effect: *Candy is bad for your teeth.* **3.** Severe or violent: *a bad storm.* **4.** Rotten or spoiled: *The milk went bad.*
**ANTONYM:** good.
**bad** (BAD) *adjective,* **worse, worst**.

**beautiful** Pleasing to look at, hear, or think about: *The sunset last night was beautiful.*
**beau•ti•ful** (BYOO tuh fuhl) *adjective.*

**bedroom** A room for sleeping: *My brother and I share a bedroom.*
**bed•room** (BED room) *noun, plural* **bedrooms**.

**before** In front of; ahead of: *We came home before dark.* Preposition.
▲ At an earlier time: *I've read this book before.* Adverb.
**be•fore** (bih FOR) *preposition; adverb.*

**begin** 1. To do the first part of something; make a start: *Begin writing now.* 2. To come into being; start: *The race will begin in five minutes.* SYNONYM: start; ANTONYMS: end, finish **be•gin** (bih GIHN) *verb,* **began, begun, beginning.**

**behind** 1. At the back of: *Jorge stood behind me in line.* 2. Later than; after: *Our bus was five minutes behind the first bus.* **be•hind** (bih HIND) *preposition.*

**below** In or to a lower place: *From the plane we could see the mountains far below.* Adverb.
▲ In a lower place than; beneath: *My friend's apartment is below mine.* Preposition.
**be•low** (bih LOH) *adverb; preposition.*

**beside** At the side of; next to: *A spider sat down beside Miss Muffet.* **be•side** (bih SID) *preposition.*

**big** Great in size; large: *We live in a big city.*

SYNONYMS: huge, large; ANTONYMS: little, small, tiny **big** (BIHG) *adjective,* **bigger, biggest.**

**birthday** The date a person was born: *We played games on my birthday.* **birth•day** (BURTH day) *noun, plural* **birthdays.**

**bitter** Having a biting, harsh, bad taste: *The coffee had a bitter taste.* **bit•ter** (BIHT uhr) *adjective.*

**blueberry** A small, dark blue, sweet berry with tiny seeds: *Blueberries grow on a shrub.* **blue•ber•ry** (BLOO ber ee) *noun, plural* **blueberries.**

**Dictionary**

**bright 1.** Giving much light; filled with light: *The sun's light is bright.* **2.** Clear; strong: *The rose was bright red.* **3.** Smart; clever: *Sandy is a bright child.* **ANTONYM:** dull. **bright** (BRIT) *adjective,* **brighter, brightest.**

**butterfly** An insect with a thin body and four large, often brightly colored wings: *I saw a yellow butterfly on a flower.* **but•ter•fly** (BUT uhr fli) *noun, plural* **butterflies**.

**careful** Paying close attention; watchful:

*Be careful when you cross the street.* **ANTONYM:** careless. **care•ful** (KAIR fuhl) *adjective.*

**clean** Free from dirt: *Put the clean dishes away.* **ANTONYM:** dirty. **clean** (KLEEN) *adjective,* **cleaner, cleanest**.

**cold 1.** Having a low temperature; not warm: *The weather is cold today.* **2.** Feeling a lack of warmth; chilly: *I was cold after playing in the snow.* **SYNONYMS:** chilly, freezing; **ANTONYMS:** hot, warm. **cold** (KOHLD) *adjective,* **colder, coldest**.

**crisp** Hard or firm but breaking easily into pieces: *Fresh celery should be crisp.* **crisp** (KRIHSP) *adjective,* **crisper, crispest**.

**crunch** To chew or crush with a noisy, crackling sound: *The cracker crunched when I bit into it.* **crunch** (KRUNCH) *verb,* **crunched, crunching**.

## D

**delicious** Pleasing or delightful to the taste or smell: *The freshly picked apples were delicious.* **de•li•cious** (dih LISH uhs) *adjective.*

**dry** Not wet or damp; with very little or no water or other liquid: *A desert is a dry place.* ANTONYM: wet. **dry** (DRI) *adjective,* **drier, driest.**

**dull 1.** Not sharp or pointed: *The knife was so dull it would not cut.* **2.** Not interesting; boring: *The book was so dull I fell asleep.* SYNONYMS: blunt, boring; ANTONYMS: interesting, sharp. **dull** (DUL) *adjective,* **duller, dullest.**

## F

**few** Not many: *I have only a few pages left to read.* ANTONYM: many. **few** (FYOO) *adjective,* **fewer, fewest.**

**finally** At the end; at last: *Baseball season is finally here!* **fi•nal•ly** (FI nuh lee) *adverb.*

**finish** To bring to an end; complete: *Finish your homework before you watch TV.* SYNONYM: end; ANTONYMS: begin, start. **fin•ish** (FIHN ihsh) *verb,* **finished, finishing.**

**first 1.** Coming before all others: *John was in the first race.* Adjective. ▲ Before anything else: *First, I do my homework, and then I play.* Adverb. ANTONYM: last. **first** (FURST) *adjective; adverb.*

**Dictionary**

**flashlight** An electric light powered by batteries and small enough to be carried. **flash•light** (FLASH lit) *noun, plural* **flashlights**.

**football 1.** A game played by two teams of eleven players each on a big field with goals at each end: *Football is a popular sport.* **2.** The oval ball used in this game: *The player carried the football across the goal line.* **foot•ball** (FÛT bawl) *noun, plural* **footballs**.

**-ful** A suffix that means: **1.** Full of: *Fearful means full of fear.* **2.** Able to; likely to: *If you are forgetful, you are likely to forget things.* **3.** The amount that will fill something: *Cupful means the amount that will fill a cup.*

**G**

**goldfish** A fish that is usually orange-gold in color, often kept in home fish tanks: *Jan has three goldfish in a tank.* **gold•fish** (GOHLD fish) *noun, plural* **goldfish**.

**good 1.** Of high quality; not bad or poor: *Kit is reading a good book.* **2.** Nice or pleasant: *Eric got good news about his uncle.* **3.** Acting properly: *My dog is good and doesn't jump on the sofa.* **ANTONYM:** bad. **good** (GÛD) *adjective,* **better, best**.

**grasshopper** A flying insect with long, powerful legs for jumping: *A grasshopper can make a chirping sound with its leg.* **grass•hop•per** (GRAS hop uhr) *noun, plural* **grasshoppers**.

**Dictionary**

## H

**happy** Feeling or showing pleasure or gladness: *Margie was happy with her good grades.* SYNONYMS: glad, joyful; ANTONYM: sad. **hap•py** (HAP ee) *adjective,* **happier, happiest.**

**hard** **1.** Solid and firm; not soft: *Loni fell and landed on the hard floor.* **2.** Difficult; not easy: *The math test was hard.* ANTONYMS: easy, soft. **hard** (HAHRD) *adjective,* **harder, hardest.**

**hot** Having a high temperature: *Don't touch the hot stove.* ANTONYM: cold. **hot** (HOT) *adjective,* **hotter, hottest.**

## I

**inside** **1.** On, in, or into the inner side or part of: *I went inside the house.* **2.** Indoors: *We played inside because it was raining.* ANTONYM: outside. **in•side** (IHN SID *or* ihn SID *or* IHN sid) *adverb.*

## K

**kind** Gentle, generous, and friendly: *Luz is kind to animals.* ANTONYM: mean. **kind** (KIND) *adjective,* **kinder, kindest.**

## L

**last** **1.** Coming after all others: *December is the last month of the year. Adjective.* ▲ After all others: *Ron came in last. Adverb.* ANTONYM: first. **last** (LAST) *adjective; adverb.*

**late** **1.** After the usual time: *Kevin was late for dinner. Adverb.* ▲ Coming near the end: *The game started in the late afternoon. Adjective.* ANTONYM: early. **late** (LAT) *adverb, adjective,* **later, latest.**

**-less** A suffix that means:
**1.** Having no; without: *Fearless means having no fear.* **2.** That cannot be: *Countless means that it cannot be counted.*

**little** **1.** Small in size or amount: *A pebble is a little stone. Adjective.* **2.** A small amount: *I wasn't hungry, so I ate only a little. Noun.* **SYNONYMS:** small, tiny; **ANTONYMS:** big, huge, large.
**lit•tle** (LIHT uhl) *adjective; noun.*

**lucky** **1.** Having or bringing good luck: *That lucky girl won first prize.* **2.** Caused by good luck: *Maria's home run was a lucky hit.*
**luck•y** (LUK ee) *adjective,* **luckier, luckiest.**

**many** **1.** Made up of a large number: *A library has many books. Adjective.* **2.** A large number: *Many of my friends came to my party. Noun.* **ANTONYM:** few.
**man•y** (MEN ee) *adjective,* **more, most**; *noun.*

**mean** Cruel; not kind or nice: *It is mean to tease a dog.* **ANTONYM:** kind.
**mean** (MEEN) *adjective,* **meaner, meanest.**

**narrow** Not wide or broad: *Andy jumped across the narrow stream.*
**nar•row** (NAR oh) *adjective,* **narrower, narrowest.**

**near** **1.** Not far or distant: *The holiday season is drawing near. Adverb.* **2.** Close to or by: *My grandparents live near the beach. Preposition.*
**near** (NIHR) *adverb,* **nearer, nearest**; *preposition.*

**new 1.** Recently grown or made: *In spring the trees have new leaves.* **2.** Not yet used or worn: *My new sneakers are so white!* ANTONYM: old. **new** (NOO) *adjective,* **newer, newest.**

**next 1.** Following in time or order: *It rained Monday, but the next day was sunny.* **2.** Nearest: *The next street is mine. Adjective.* ▲ Immediately after: *Read this book next. Adverb.* **next** (NEKST) *adjective; adverb.*

**noisy** Making much noise: *The noisy children had to leave the library.* ANTONYM: quiet. **nois•y** (NOY zee) *adjective,* **noisier, noisiest.**

**now 1.** At this time: *I am sitting at my desk now.* **2.** Immediately: *Do your homework now.* **now** (NOW) *adverb.*

— **o** —

**old 1.** Having existed for a long time: *That castle is very old.*

**2.** Of a certain age: *Enrique is seven years old.* ANTONYMS: new, young. **old** (OHLD) *adjective,* **older, oldest.**

**opposite 1.** On the other side of or across from: *Leon lives on the opposite side of the street from me.* **2.** Turned or moving the other way: *We passed a car going in the opposite direction. Adjective.* ▲ Something that is completely different from another: *Hot is the opposite of cold. Noun.* **op•po•site** (OP uh ziht) *adjective; noun, plural* **opposites.**

**Dictionary**

**outside** The outer side, surface, or part: *The outside of the house needs painting. Noun.*
▲ Outdoors: *We played outside all day. Adverb.* **ANTONYM:** inside.
**out•side** (OWT SID *or* owt SID or OWT sid) *noun; adverb.*

**P**

**pale** Not bright in color: *The rose was a pale pink.* **pale** (PAYL) *adjective,* **paler, palest.**

**Q**

**quarter** **1.** One of four equal parts: *Fifteen minutes is a quarter of an hour.* **2.** A coin worth 25 cents: *There are four quarters in a dollar.* **quar•ter** (KWAWR tuhr) *noun, plural* **quarters.**

**quiet** Making little or no noise: *It is always quiet in the library.* **ANTONYMS:** loud, noisy.
**qui•et** (KWI it) *adjective,* **quieter, quietest.**

**R**

**rainbow** A curve of colored light seen in the sky: *A rainbow is caused by the sun's shining through drops of water in the air.* **rain•bow** (RAYN boh) *noun, plural* **rainbows.**

**re-** A prefix that means: **1.** Again: *Refill means to fill again.* **2.** Back: *Recall means to call back.*

**S**

**sad** Unhappy: *Fern was sad when her best friend moved away.* ANTONYMS: glad, happy. **sad** (SAD) *adjective*, **sadder, saddest**.

**sailboat** A boat that is moved by the wind blowing against its sail or sails: *The sailboat flew across the water.* **sail•boat** (SAYL boht) *noun, plural* **sailboats**.

**seashell** The shell of a clam or other sea animal: *Ella found a pretty seashell on the beach.* **sea•shell** (SEE shel) *noun, plural* **seashells**.

**shiny** Shining; bright: *The new penny was shiny.* ANTONYM: dull. **shin•y** (SHI nee) *adjective*, **shinier, shiniest**.

**short** Not long or tall: *Ken got a very short haircut.* ANTONYM: tall. **short** (SHORT) *adjective*, **shorter, shortest**.

**sleepy** Ready for or needing sleep: *I take a nap when I feel sleepy.* SYNONYM: tired. **sleep•y** (SLEE pee) *adjective*, **sleepier, sleepiest**.

**small** Not large; little: *A mouse is a small animal.* SYNONYMS: little, tiny; ANTONYMS: big, huge, large. **small** (SMAWL) *adjective*, **smaller, smallest**.

**soft** 1. Easy to shape; not hard: *Pete rolled the soft clay into a ball.* 2. Smooth to the touch: *A baby has soft skin.* 3. Gentle or light; not harsh: *Lia has a soft voice.* ANTONYM: hard. **soft** (SOFT) *adjective*, **softer, softest**.

**Dictionary**

**soon 1.** In a short time: *Come see us again* **soon**. **2.** Early: *Our guests came too* **soon**. **3.** Quickly: *I'll be there as* **soon** *as I can*. **soon** (SOON) *adverb*.

**start 1.** To begin to act, move, or happen: *Let's start the game now*. **2.** To make something act, move, or happen: *You turn the key to* **start** *the car*. ANTONYMS: end, finish. **start** (STAHRT) *verb*, **started, starting**.

**sunflower** A large flower that grows on a tall plant: *A* **sunflower** *has a brown center and yellow petals*. **sun•flow•er** (SUN flow uhr) *noun*, *plural* **sunflowers**.

**sunlight** The light of the sun: *The* **sunlight** *warmed our faces*. **sun•light** (SUN lit) *noun*.

**tall 1.** Higher than average; not short or low: *Chicago has many* **tall** *buildings*. **2.** Having a certain height: *Jack is four feet* **tall**. ANTONYM: short. **tall** (TAWL) *adjective*, **taller, tallest**.

**tame 1.** Taken from the wild state and made gentle or obedient: **Tame** *elephants walked in the circus parade*. **2.** Not fearful or shy: *The birds were* **tame** *enough to eat out of my hand*. ANTONYM: wild. **tame** (TAYM) *adjective*, **tamer, tamest**.

**today 1.** The present day or time: *Is* **today** *a school day? Noun* **2.** On or during the present day: *Do you want to go bike riding* **today**? *Adverb*. **to•day** (tuh DAY) *noun*; *adverb*.

**tomorrow** The day after today: *Today is Friday, so tomorrow will be Saturday.* Noun.
▲ On the day after today: *We're going to the beach tomorrow.* Adverb.
**to•mor•row** (tuh MOR oh) *noun; adverb.*

**un-** A prefix that means: **1.** Not: *Uncooked means not cooked.* **2.** To do the opposite of: *Unlock means to do the opposite of lock.*

**waterfall** A stream of water falling from a high place: *Take a picture of the lovely waterfall.*
**wa•ter•fall** (WAW tuhr fawl) *noun, plural* **waterfalls**.

**wet** Covered, soaked, or damp with water or other liquid: *My hair was wet from the rain.*
SYNONYMS: damp, moist;
ANTONYM: dry.
**wet** (WET) *adjective,* **wetter, wettest**.

**wild** Not controlled by people; living or growing in nature: *A raccoon is a wild animal.*
ANTONYM: tame.
**wild** (WILD) *adjective,* **wilder, wildest**.

**yesterday 1.** The day before today: *Yesterday was a holiday.* **2.** On the day before today: *I just started this book yesterday.*
**yes•ter•day** (YES tuhr day) *noun; adverb.*

**young** In the early part of life or growth; not old: *A lamb is a young sheep.*
ANTONYM: old.
**young** (YUNG) *adjective,* **younger, youngest**.

**Index**

501

**Index**

504

Index

Index

# ACKNOWLEDGMENTS

**The publisher gratefully acknowledges permission to reprint the following copyrighted material:**

"Apt. 3" from *Apt.3* by Ezra Jack Keats. Copyright © 1971 by Ezra Jack Keats. Reprinted by permission of Aladdin Books.

"August Heat" from *Read-Aloud Rhymes for the Very Young* selected by Jack Prelutsky. Copyright ©1986 by Alfred A. Knopf, Inc.

"Fossils Tell of Long Ago" from *Fossils Tell of Long Ago* by Aliki. Copyright © 1972, 1990 by Aliki Brandenberg. Reprinted by permission of Harper Trophy, a division of HarperCollins Publishers.

"Higher on the Door" from *Higher on the Door* by James Stevenson. Copyright © 1987 by James Stevenson. Reprinted by permission of Greenwillow Books.

"Jamaica Tag-Along" from *Jamaica Tag-Along* by Juanita Havill. Text copyright © 1989 by Juanita Havill. Illustrations copyright © 1989 by Anne Sibley O'Brien. Reprinted by permission of Houghton Mifflin Company. All rights reserved.

"Night Animal, Day Animal" by Judith Lechner. Copyright © McGraw-Hill School Division.

"The Relatives Came" from *The Relatives Came* by Cynthia Rylant. Text copyright © 1985 Cynthia Rylant. Reprinted with the permission of Simon & Schuster Books for Young Readers, an imprint of Simon & Schuster Children's Publishing Division.

"Swimmy" from *Swimmy* by Leo Lionni. Copyright © 1963 by Leo Lionni. Reprinted by permission of Pantheon Books, a division of Random House, Inc.

"Tomás and the Library Lady" from *Tomás and the Library Lady* by Pat Mora. Text copyright © 1997 by Pat Mora. Illustrations copyright © 1997 by Raul Colón. Reprinted by permission of Alfred A. Knopf, Inc.

"When I Was Young in the Mountains" from *When I Was Young in the Mountains* by Cynthia Rylant, copyright © 1982 by Cynthia Rylant. Used by permission of Dutton Children's Books, a division of Penguin Putnam Inc.

"Which?" by James S. Tippett from *Crickety Cricket! The Best-Loved Poems of James S. Tippett.* Text copyright © 1973 by Martha K. Tippett. Reprinted by permission of HarperCollins Publishers.

"Zipping, Zapping, Zooming Bats" from *Zipping, Zapping, Zooming Bats* by Ann Earle. Text copyright © 1995 by Ann Earle. Illustrations copyright © 1995 by Henry Cole. Reprinted by permission of HarperCollins Children's Books, a division of HarperCollins Publishers.

**Cover Design and Illustration:** Robert Brook Allen
**Cover Photo:** Gary Buss/FPG International

ILLUSTRATION CREDITS: Daniel DelValle, 49, 49, 51, 119, 189, 261, 397. Lou Pappas 329, 395.

PHOTO CREDITS: All Stock-Picture Quest: Charles Krebs 343. Animals Animals: Joe McDonald 258. Art Resource: Werner Forman 399. Beaura Ringrose: 224, 399. Bob Daemmrich: 219, 220, 339. Bruce Coleman Inc.: James Blank 43; Jane Burton 142; Bob and Clara Calhoun 273; Robert Carr 156; D. Donadoni 137; Wendell Metzen 259; Jack Montgomery 268; M. Timothy O'Keefe 7; Hans Reinhard 409; Lee Rentz 487. Corbis: 320, 356, 357; Bruce Burkhardt 148, Joseph-Siffred Duplessis 324. David R. Frazier Photolibrary: 275, 286, 486; Aaron Haupt 9. DRK Photo: John Cancalosi 314; Steve Kaufman 46; Stephen J. Kraseman 246; Pat O'Hara 112; Barbara Cushman Ro Rowell 94; Larry Ulrich 1, 131; Don and Pat Valenti 272. Earth Scenes: Patti Murray 119. EyeWire Inc.: Digital Vision 259. FPG International: 288; Paul Avis 137; Jose Luis Banus-March 225; Ken Chernus 373; Jim Cummins 186, 267, 488; Tony Miller 375. H. Armstrong Roberts, Inc.: Richard Fukuhara 197. Hutchings Photography: T2, T4, T6, T10, T13, T14, T17, 12, 38, 40, 44, 48, 49, 50, 108, 110, 114, 118, 120, 129, 141, 143, 148, 154, 176, 178, 182, 186, 188, 248, 250, 254, 258, 260, 289, 316, 318, 322, 326, 328, 337, 344, 384, 386, 390, 398, 400, 407. Image Bank 81, Erlanson Productions Impact Visuals 341. Index Stock Imagery: Scott Shapiro 130. Index Stock Photography Inc.: 201, 343, 482. Lawrence Migdale 78, 163, 381. MMSD 355; Ken Cavanagh 149; Ken Karp 135; Bob Randall 196; Francis Westfield 5. Monkmeyer: Pat Farley 347. Panoramic Images: Paul Chandris 410; Jeff Lepore 402, Bruce McNitt 12, James Schwabel 290. Peter Arnold Inc.:C & M Denis-Huot 26; John Kieffer 271; Gerard Lacz 358; NASA 354. Photo Edit: 296; Bill Bachmann 212; Gary A. Conner 14, 346; Myrleen Ferguson 2, 59, 65, 99, 103, 171, 175, 245, 280; Tony Freeman 33, 35, 60, 72, 153, 327, 379; Robert Ginn 313; Spencer Grant 326; Will Hart 277; Richard Hutchings 283; John Neubauer 27; Michael Newman 15, 56, 105, 243, 266, 361, 489; Alan Oddie 491; D.A. Ramey 74; David Young-Wolff 57, 69, 73, 186, 194, 199, 216, 226, 284, 379, 412, 494. Photo Researchers, Inc.: 171; Ron Church 282; Ray Coleman 406; Gregory G. Dimijian 208; Richard Hutchings 70, 144, 281; Tom and Pat Leeson 258; Renee Lynn 285; Maslowski 128; Susan McCartney 404; Tom McHugh 239; Lawrence Migdale 222; Rod Planck 270; J. H. Robinson 406; Gregory K. Scott 224; Lee F. Snyder 276; Jim Steinberg 495; Jerry Wachter 152; Jim Weiner 340; F. Stuart Westmorland 382. Photodisc: 16, 18, 58, 68, 132, 134, 184, 200, 202, 252, 256, 275, 336, 348. Picture Quest 6, 292. Rainbow: Coco McCoy 36, B. & J. McGrath 307. Stock • Boston: 11, 221; J. Cancalosi 234; Bob Daemmrich 11, 33; Frank Siteman 29. Stock • Boston-Picture Quest: Eric Neurath 218. SuperStock: 3, 25, 61, 75, 77, 80, 121, 126, 129, 142, 164, 187, 243, 327, 350, 353, 370, 371, 405, 408, 484, 493; A.K.G., Berlin 326; Leslie Braddock 310; Collection of Gregory Erwin/Jane Wooster Scott 32; Christian Pierre 242; Lance Richbourg 378. The Bridgeman Art Library: Patricia Espir 170; Dora Holzhandler 102. The Granger Collection Rembrandt Peale 291. The Image Works: Bill Bachmann 213; Tom Brakefield 303; Bob Daemmrich 33, 71, 218; Townsend P. Dickinson 24; Jacksonville Journal Courier 152; James Marshall 88; Yva Momatiuk and John Eastcott 492; Okoniewski 145; Tim Reese 311. The Stock Market: 311; Roger Ball 138; Paul Barton 490; Ed Bock 294; Tom Brakefield 302; Anthony Edgeworth 360; Joe Feingersh 150; Charles Gupton 83; John Henley 165; Henley and Savage 278; Ted Horowitz 147; John Madere 304; Rob Matheson 210; Jeffrey Myers 127; Robert Ono 96; Jose L. Pelaez 151, 203, 398; Zefa Reinhard 118; Norbert Schäfer 348, 352; George Schiavone 362; Ariel Skelley 82, 167, 214, 485; William Waterfall 293. Tony Stone Images: 195; 215; Amwell 28; Dan Bosler 140; Rick Burton 48; Laurie Campbell 119; Cosmo Condina 63; Kate Connell 64; Daniel J. Cox 116, 351, 359; Bob Daemmrich 236; Tim Davis 305, 364; Philipp Engelhorn 173; Ken Fisher 372; David Hanover 64; Alan Hicks 106; Klaus Lahnstein 10; Vito Palmisano 235; Peter Pearson 4; Lori Adamski Peek 103; Greg Probst 403; John Riley 413; Hugh Sitton 84; Karen Su 359; Mike Timo 211; Keith Wood 85.